AF348704

From the Heart of a Naturalist

jules talarico

edited by tess julianna

A Russian Hill Press Book
United States • United Kingdom • Australia

Russian Hill Press

The publisher is not responsible for websites or their content that are not owned by the publisher.

ISBN: 978-1-7378246-1-9
Library of Congress Control Number: 2022902827

Cover designed by Deboarh Bernal with Dragon Wing Publising

To Joanne, my wife, for the freedom you gave to me to travel and experience the world of nature … to my boots for the journeys you took me on … and finally, to Anna for helping me put this dream into print.

Written by my wife Joanne to Jules

Like a gift it is,
   this magic of viewing
   a mountain top,
   a lake, a tree.
A special giving of
   God to man.
No returns required,
   the gift is the forever
   flow of a short breath,
   a tear, a heartbeat
   out-of-step.
You tie your boot laces
   and greet a new day,
   thankful for living.
Your dad would say,
   Look over there Jul," the smile
   in his eyes to match the
   splendor of the mountain
   crest.
You tie a lot in those laces.
The strong legs and feet of
   a thousand steps,
Steps taken and shared
   with thoughts of him
   who always remains as
   beautiful as that mountain
   crest.
Gift it is, to take the part
   of him along …
   the special part, the love and wonder that
   supports, ties together the

grace of God in nature.
A gift it is, the knowing and
  sensing his presence at each
  new view.
Like eons of nature's work and
  growth, his spirit expands
  beyond the Canyon …
  to the mountain, the lake, the tree.
Every new step of the way
  this gift glows of a shared
  love and memory.

Joanne Talarico
June 23, 1982

Contents

Introduction

journeys… we all take them… i wonder, can life be considered one long journey, or just a multitude of smaller ones… and at the end of a given journey, always lies the destination… is that what we seek, or is it something different… something that will feed your soul and spirit for the years to come…

over the past hundreds of years, thousands of voyagers have walked Camino de Santiago, a pilgrimage also known as The Way of St. James is the sole purpose of this pilgrimage is to reach the Cathedral of Santiago de Compostela in Galicia, Spain… no, for a pilgrimage can be defined as a journey or more importantly a search of moral or spiritual significance… what one finds and gains everyday from that experience, that is the reward one carries with them for the rest of their life, not the final steps to a specific destination… no, they are soon forgotten and what of my life's journeys.

Preface

we wander through life at times without a known direction, just drifting until that direction is found… after graduating from high school, it was just assumed that college was my next stepping stone in life… i had no idea of what major or career would be of interest, but regardless, college was the smartest choice to pursue, as the Viet Nam War was in full force… North Viet Nam had just launched the Tet Offensive and the death count was climbing… the horror and ugliness of war became a reality, thanks to the nightly news with Walter Cronkite showing boys just like me dying every night right before our eyes on TV…

it seems that throughout time, parents especially fathers, wanted their sons to achieve everything they couldn't, for the son to have every opportunity available that had been denied the father, yet there were those experiences most fathers did not want their sons to endure, such as the horror of war and watching friends die… to avoid being drafted into the army during the Viet Nam War, many boys like me were encouraged to enroll in college…

my grades from high school really put a limit on what colleges would want to take a chance with an academically-at-risk kid… in a strange way, and because the school that finally decided to accept me was closed down due to violating segregation guidelines, i ended up on the campus of Old Dominion College, which had the reputation of the party school of Virginia…

exactly four semesters and one week were spent as a student on that campus, changing my major every other semester, from Psychology all the way to Army ROTC… test to qualify and enter into the ROTC program as a third-year cadet, i failed the required, therefore keeping an academic record as a failure intact… with my academic world falling apart, i simply walked out of an astronomy class in the first week of my third fall semester and withdrew from college… i earned only 17 semester credit hours during that time, proving that college was not part of my future… dropping out of college meant losing my student deferment, but by this time a lottery system was in place for drafting boys into the jungles of Viet Nam… i felt lucky - my draft number was 305, well into the zone of "you'll never have to worry about being drafted"…

after a year was spent drifting from a handful of useless jobs, a decision was made to join the U. S. Air Force as an Air Traffic Controller… then in a twisted way, a remote assignment to Thailand was swapped for one in Greenland, and without knowing it, i finally found a direction in life… the geology of Greenland had me do something that i had never been done before, putting on a pair of hiking boots and starting to hike and experience the world of nature and the geology of Greenland… i now had a direction and goal in life, to become a geologist…

my next assignment after Greenland was Luke Air Force Base near Phoenix, Arizona… being four hours from the Grand Canyon and its incredible geology along with living in the Sonoran Desert only helped increase an interest in geology and a love for the natural world… in my remaining time in the service, an Associate Degree was earned with an emphasis in geology…

also of importance, as it affected not only how i viewed the natural world but values i would hold on to in the coming years, my wife, a high school English teacher, introduced me to the works of Henry David Thoreau, Ralph Waldo Emerson, Samuel Taylor Coleridge and William Cullen Bryant… from my time hiking in Yosemite and the Sierra, i not only read the writings of both John Muir and John Burroughs, but i became a disciple of their beliefs that nature can heal the soul of man…

three years after an honorable discharge, a degree in geology was earned at Arizona State University, and a love for the world of academia was forming… being qualified as a geologist was a line of work where hiking boots were essential, unfortunately just prior to graduating, the job market in geology collapsed, so a decision was now made to follow the career path of my wife as a high school teacher, but in a field that had become a big part of my life, geology… hiking boots now became a way to bring my experiences with geology and the natural world into the classroom… more and more time was being spent hiking, backpacking, and exploring, in order to understand the geology and ecology of Arizona, and then to bring that knowledge to my students… i never stopped going to school though…   after earning a Master's Degree in Science Education, another 60 graduate hours in biology taken, including doing original research on the desert tortoise… there was always an urge to learn something new and hike somewhere my boots had never been to…

we get gifts from our parents that we aren't really aware of as we are growing up and maturing… my father gave me the gift of seeing and appreciating nature at its fullest… i will never forget the joy in my father's eyes and the beauty of his words as i took him into a dream of his life, a mule trip into the Grand Canyon… a million questions he asked about aspects of this canyon that had just become a large part of my life… with his beloved binoculars, my father could look at an eagle or raven in flight for hours with that beautiful smile in his eyes… a cloud was more than just a cloud in the sky… that gift was given to me as i now journeyed through the world of nature… a hike in an old growth forest had me just like a child, my hands touching the bark of every giant i walked by, my neck straining to look upward towards the heavens to see the canopy of this forest… i would use every sense i was blessed with, listening, smelling and touching the world my boots had taken me into… this habit has never left me but instead bestowed upon me so many beautiful moments, moments that had to be remembered…
it was my mother, i like to think, who gave me the gift of reading… as a small child i remember my mother walking me and my sister to

the Audubon Library to pick out books… books became an escape for me and a way to explore adventures i hoped would someday be a part of my life… i can fondly remember picking up two books in a book trailer that came to my school, *Billy Budd* and *Two Years Before the Mast*… little did i know that i was being drawn into a love affair with the sea… the love of the sea was another gift bestowed upon me by my mother… today one of my most prized and loved possessions is my very own library… tens of thousands of pages that have felt my fingers as i journeyed through each and every one of my books…

my mother also gave me my gift of writing… my mother journaled her way through life as her writing became a means to battle and understand all the demons in her life… as i grew older and started to write my thoughts, my mother was always there to encourage me to write more and more… slowly the pages accumulated in folders and eventually into journals… every time i tied on my hiking books to explore the world that i was so deeply drawn to, a journal was always with me to record my thoughts… on the summits of mountains, the canyons of Arizona, kayaking coastal shores, sailing my beloved sailboat Tranquility, all the way to my years as a Naturalist with Princess Cruises, my journals were always with me… today my journals can be found in a special place on a bookshelf in my library…

From the Heart of a Naturalist is a small collection of many of my journeys… a summer in Alaska with Princess Cruises… trails my boots have walked on throughout my life… i tried to include entries from all the different journeys my boots have taken me on, and even included ones where my boots were replaced by a kayak paddle and finally to the beautiful white sails of Tranquility as we danced across the San Diego Bay…
the pages that follow are my thoughts, lessons i learned, my hopes, the happiness and the beliefs i have attained from nature to heal my

soul... these essays came from my heart and reveal many of the values that made me the person i am today... the person that i became because of the boots that i wore on so many journeys...

these writings were both experienced and written by jules, but i owe it to tess who finally put these words to press... the story of jules and tess will hopefully follow soon and will be written solely by tess...

it's once been said a journey begins with the first step taken... these are my first steps, come walk with me.

jules

Part 1

Tidal Ebbing: Reflections of an Alaskan Summer

May 13, 2014
Sun City West, AZ
Bittersweet Feelings

my bags are slowly swelling, still half-filled suitcases lay scattered about… it's been warm here in Phoenix recently so it seems strange to be packing flannel shirts, sweatshirts, bluejeans, and even jackets and gloves… i keep revising my list from last year, what did i need that i didn't have… i've already shipped one box of books up to Alaska and as i look at the weight slowly accumulating in my bags, i know i should have mailed at least two more boxes…

and as i slowly pack my world into bags, i keep seeing his brown eyes, worried and he knows his best friend will be leaving… it's not easy leaving for almost 5 months… Joanne understands, we'll put the money aside for days that we'll travel throughout Italy… but how do you explain or justify your absence to a golden retriever? you can't, and it breaks my heart to know for weeks he'll wait, looking out the window for his friend to return… yes, he'll drag the clothes i left behind with my scent… i wonder does it make it any easier for him… i hope so… yet it seems he is slowly preparing for me to leave as he's not always by my side, my shadow… no, he sits across the room, but always i'm within his view…

leaving Tranquility, my 30' Catalina sloop berthed in San Diego, was hard… walking away from her berth, knowing it would be months before i filled her sails with the wind… it's in that instant, when the engine is shut down and the wind catches the sails, Tranquility comes alive as she lets the wind heel her over… the water rushes by her hull and fills your ears with a symphony of joy as you can sense her desire to dance across the waters… ah, i love the wind in my face and the salt in my beard and there by my side, always my companion, Joshua… did he enjoy these moments as i did, i wonder, or was just being by my side all he wanted… Tranquility now sits a day away from these open suitcases… scatterings of clothes, books and my boots waiting to be packed …. i hope that she waits silently… i know i will also have to wait for my hands to once again caress her soul… will she know i'll carry her in my thoughts all through this summer that we're apart…

and of Joanne… my honey-do lists are almost finished… Joshua will be her shadow now, her best friend… and even though i have yet to leave, i miss her touch, her scent, the crazy little things that have made her an intimate part of my life for the past 42 years… and all i can do is to count the days till she joins me up in Alaska, till her hand is held in mine once again…

this summer the Island Princess will be my little Walden Pond… i have brought many books i've been wanting to read, some that i must reread… it took time to build the piles of books… and i think too of the many books i read to prepare for Alaska once again… i found at least a dozen great reads that i enjoyed this winter, and now i'm anxious to see these places… their stories left unfinished in my mind… it should be a good summer of reading filled with quiet moments as i sit with my mug of hot tea and Alaska slowly passing by…

and i think, yes… soon i'll be with the whales once again…. the cold, damp wind in my face… it will probably be cloudy and maybe even some rain… will i see the female i saw in Hawaii this winter with her newborn calf… will they have made the journey safely… she'll be happy to feed on the krill and especially the oil rich herring after all those months without food… her calf will stay close to her in the beginning of the summer… it will be a summer of learning, preparing for a cycle that will continue throughout its life… never questioning, just responding to an internal feeling, one that at first she'll not understand…

ah to see the eagles… my ravens… to enjoy my walks **in** the forest… the silence, the smells… my hands always touching…. my camera always by my side, painting the pictures of my summer in this land of the gentle giants decorated with the berries and wildflowers… yes, it should be a good summer…

i pause in thought as i struggle to choose something to fill another empty spot in the suitcase… a parade of thoughts will fill my mind these next two days… they will all be bittersweet… life is a lot like that too…

May 15, 2014
Written aboard the Island Princess

with bags in tow, i hesitated as i prepared to walk out the door… it never gets any easier saying good-bye… you can never express what you want to say in those fleeting minutes… a waiting taxi… everything is a rush now… i hold her one more time and know i will miss her dearly, but how do i say good-bye to Joshua… early this morning we walked as we do every day, yet i sensed he knew it would be awhile before we shared this walk again… i sat on our sofa and petted him as i looked into his big sorrowful brown eyes… what would he say if he could… throughout our summer separation Joanne and i know that phone calls will now have to be our lifeline… we will depend on those phone calls to hold on to our lives together… only a day into my summer Joanne told me of his upset stomach and how he refuses to leave his window seat hoping i will, but knowing i probably won't, be home tonight to walk him once again….

i know it wasn't any easier for her… do i really know the pain she feels as we part again… her lonely thoughts of our time spent hand in hand… our little day trips…. talks around the table…. holding her hand as we say grace… at times i wonder is it really worth it… my boots have taken me down many paths during these years and she has always encouraged me… she knows what the sea, mountains, and canyons mean to me

i reflect on last summer… images come flooding back… the glaciers, the forest, friends i'll see once again and my whales…

16 July 2013
Leaving Alaska

i got the wind to my back with a following sea, the sky is blue with fair winds and good weather predicted… yet i sadly sail southbound…

behind i left the many days of my Alaskan summer… Queen Charlotte Island sliding pass on our starboard side throughout the silence of the night… the joy of blue water in our passage down to Vancouver Island… onward and homeward bound…
it was only yesterday afternoon that i once again boarded in my little haven called Ketchikan, yet i hesitated as if i could delay what i had to do…

"Take me back to Ketchikan where i'll be a happy man" and as i sat with her, Joanne, my solid rock… she knew my thoughts as i watched the dock slowly slip away… my future coming into focus and my past fading… it's always hard to let go what you know and have enjoyed…. my future like the weather, so uncertain… but i believe it will be full of sunshine…

the green of the Tongass forest paraded by slowly as i once again wandered in my thoughts up Deer Mountain and the loop along the Chilkoot that i have walked so many times in the past summers… i can't describe the softness of the forest, its tranquility… the massive trees, sentinels in this fortress, guardians of a solitude that i am always drawn to…. the moss, lichen, the song of the ravens… how many times did i stop like a child to admire, my hands always touching, my eyes always discovering, my ears always listening to the solitude that only the forest can feel… many times the path was muddy as my boots slowly carried me on… sadly those boots now are tucked away in a closet, waiting to be packed… i remember the snow on Deer Mountain and the rain as it fell…. my disappointment is there were too few rainy days this summer to splash through the puddles like a child and feel the rain… it was only yesterday that i walked a familiar walk with a friend, stopping to taste the berries, the fireweed's blooms slowly making their way to the top only to soon fade as the cotton takes to seed… i'll miss that this summer along with the first snows… termination dust is what my Alaskan friends call that first snow, remember that rock quarry by the side of the road, our hands fumbling though the debris looking for treasures… i'll miss you Ketchikan…. and your boats…. God i loved watching the boats always parading by… thinking of the fishermen, the salt in their beards and the ocean… a hell of a way to make a living in a paradise that can turn to shit in a second, yet once it's in your blood its hard to leave…

and to you, Juneau

it was my time with my gentle giants, Rachel's whales… how lucky she is… and to those friends that i shared the company of the whales with, i'll have to wait till next summer to see your smiles and hear your laughter… life would be a prison without memories, so i'll always have those moments to enjoy… and to my whales… the sound of your blow, anticipating your dive and just being out there in your company…. the bubble-net feeding…. to what gods must i thank for these moments… funny after a while i took all those moments for granted only to really appreciate them when they were no longer… but i have my photos… those frozen minutes that i'll always relish… damn i love Alaska… and my Arizona skies won't be blessed with your ravens, their chants and songs… the eagles… no, soon i'll feel the heat of the desert sun once again…

and to Haines… my heart will always be there with the Chilkalt Mountains… your fortress walls that frame my little paradise… since that summer in 1989, i spoke your name always with fondness… and to all of my friends there, hell it's hardest to say goodbye to you… thank you for your friendship and for all you taught me in the forest… i always listened like a child, while my eyes danced about the trees, trying to soak up the forest… the bears were elusive this summer but that was part of the journey… i understood their solitude…

and finally to the many faces that were a part of my everyday… thank you, for you made me smile when i didn't have what i so dearly miss with me everyday… Joanne is by my side today and soon my boy Joshua will be also… hopefully never to leave… but to all of you… thank you for your friendship
(the present, on the Island Princess)…

my feelings, parading every which way, an emotional roller coaster… i will miss Joanne and Joshua dearly all summer long, yet i still hear Alaska calling in so many ways…

i sit alone, watching California pass slowly by… i choose to eat alone tonight even though the tables are full and the chatter is with adventure… but for me, tonight i'll keep company with my thoughts of those i left behind…

> but now it comes to distances and
> both of us must try
> your eyes are soft with sorrow
> hey that's no way to say good-bye
>
> Leonard Cohen

there's never a right way to say good bye to those who mean the world to you…

May 17 2014
Somewhere off the coast of Southern California
i awoke to misty skies and a sea alive with whitecaps… northward we're bound to Alaska or should i say we're in a northward bash up the California coast…. our ship ploughs against the wind and current as we struggle up the coast towards San Francisco… this may be the last sea day that my shorts are worn, and i'm sure wearing my vest or jacket will be a daily occurrence for many days to come… it feels good to feel that chilly, damp air in my face once again….

my world feels the rhythm of the sea once again… today it's gentle, but i pray the sea becomes more alive… a little whistling in the wind would be nice… the sea is painted a deep gray in color…

later today and thru the evening we shall sail by the coast of Big Sur… i remember fondly the many times driving that coast, i would look out to sea wishing i was there… sadly i can't see the coast in these passing moments, its blanket of trees, the gentle giants that stand guardian along this coast… it's always a good walk under that carpet of gentle giants… sadly my heart knows that i may have to wait until yet another journey for my boots to walk that forest again…

this evening the clouds hang low to the horizon…. there will be no sunset to watch tonight and the winds are getting more of a bite to them as the chill slides right through my heavy sweatshirt… i walk the decks as i stand my watch over the sea… soon the moon shall rise and steal the pitch dark of night away… will there be stars to gaze at tonight, i wonder…

it was a good day… but still i feel that ache of love from those that i left behind… hopefully i feel it for many a days…

May 18, 2014
Muir Woods, California

today i took a walk with the spirit of John Muir as i wandered amongst his redwood trees… it's an area that was protected, preserved and finally made into a National Park, Muir Woods…

"the mountains are calling and i must go", it's been so long since i walked among these silent giants… i promise myself repeatedly that i will hike Yosemite and King's Canyon once again… as i walked slowly down this path memories come flooding back of past hikes through the redwood forests and its solitude… i remember my hands were always touching… i would stop and smell the bark of the trees… arching my head back so i could see these giants rising upward into the fog… picking up cones of the Sequoia, Redwood, Sugar Pines, and Douglas fir… at times i would just stop as there was no need to cover any given distance… but it's today and i am far from those memories… i was alone today, as the crowds took to the straight and level, while i found a path that climbed upward with only my boots as my companion… it was the path well chosen as for most of the time it was only me and these giants… trees that were hundreds and some maybe even a thousand years old…. monuments of creation…. a forest cathedral... Muir saw nature as the masterpiece of his creator… i stopped often… a silent prayer of thanks… a prayer of praise…

later in a gale of wind, we crossed under the Golden Gate Bridge to head northbound… once again the ocean was alive and full of spit… i couldn't help but think the next time i cross under this bridge my soul will be filled with memories of Alaska and in my heart i will know my journey is ending and once again i'll be in her arms and Joshua will be by my side… until then… Alaska calls…

May 20, 2014
Victoria, British Columbia

it was a sunny day…. not much of a wind and the Straits of Juan De Fuca were not too rough for our inbound passage… i arrived in Victoria in the afternoon and would be there till late evening with only one thing on my mind, the orcas of the San Juan Islands...

as we headed out, my hopes were high to see the orcas once again, but really it was just good to be in the waters of these orca pods again… if i saw the orcas it would just be icing on the cake… talking with the boat's naturalist, i learned that we would probably be seeing a transient pod as they have been in the area lately… residential orcas prey on fish and that means salmon, but it seems the Canadian stock of salmon numbers are low now, so the residential pods are moving more than usual… the political battle of a sustainable population of salmon between the commercial fishermen and the orcas is ongoing, and it seems at this time the orcas are on the losing side…

heading out, the wind felt refreshing on my face and the chill in the air, well it wasn't too bad… my eyes were dancing across the waters, continually searching for that tall dorsal fin… marine biologists refer to the mature male's dorsal fin as a witches hat… finally i saw them, and with my camera in hand i aimed, hopeful for that great photo, but it didn't really matter… i realized long ago that sometimes trying for that photo isn't really worth it as i miss so much of what is happening around me…. the big picture can't be experienced when one is stuck looking through the viewfinder of a camera…. today my photos were few, but my memory recorded so much more… yes, it was a good day…

and tomorrow, well it will be the start of my Alaskan summer…

May 23
Ketchikan, Alaska

Take me back to Ketchikan
That's where I'll be a happy man…
We'll find a little peace up on Garden Lane
Take me back to Ketchikan
That's where I'll be a happy man

Dennis Doyle

yesterday was cold, wet, and windy due to a good low pressure system bringing plenty of rain… walking the deck of the ship i now call my home, i could feel the wind was a biting one which slammed right into my bearded face, and the chill, well it felt good… and as the rain fell on my face, it felt good as it cleansed me, washing away all the remaining desert dust… the sea was alive today with a good following sea and the swells were building slowly to nearly 10 feet… i thought of my brother… i could imagine us sailing these waters… there would be laughter in the wind… our foul weather gear wet from the green water washing over us… we would probably be fighting for who should be at the helm…. i would yell, "Jeff that last gust of wind was over 50 knots"… he would then demand for his time at the helm… but respect for the sea we both do share… and then, to my displeasure, slowly the grey, foggy skies began to show a hint of clearing…

i was heading to north to Ketchikan, Alaska... my favorite little town and i know not why… maybe because i enjoyed so many beautiful rainy days there…. would this clearing sky be an omen that no rain would grace my tomorrow…

talking to my wife on the phone I am told some sad and disturbing news…. a friend of ours, out of the blue, a nagging cough turned into stage four cancer with only days, not even weeks, to live… it hit me like a truck… how fragile life really is, and i mean that… it made me stop and think, promise myself to be grateful for what i have and not ever to take a sunset for granted… to stop and always embrace the moment… feel the wind on my beard… really feel it…. to take life slower, for i know not when my travels will end for whatever reason…

and yes, back to Ketchikan… it was a beautiful sunny day today…. but as i walked the streets i told myself… no i promised myself… that a winter will soon pass with me in my little town of Ketchikan... a cold and wet winter i would ask for with a good fire and a pile of books… life is too short…

after leaving Ketchikan this afternoon we headed northward for our sail through Snow Passage … as the coastline slowly crept closer, it was obvious we were about to pass through Snow Passage… earlier in the day i told the passengers of my many journeys through this area and the whales that i had seen…. as the minutes pass and we sailed cautiously northward we waited patiently in solitude for the whales that i promised would be there… we waited and waited… a prayer was answered as a whale breached right in front of us… i thought of my friend and the agony of his final days and in that moment that breach meant the world to me… it was my sunset and goodbye to a dear friend…

May 24, 2014
Juneau, Alaska

Juneau… that means only one thing… today i get to spend the day in the company of my gentle giants of the sea… i'll have the wind in my beard, the smell of salt water and the mountains in the background… i don't care if it's rainy or sunny… all that doesn't matter… i just want to be amongst the whales…

as we headed out from Auk Bay we were treated right away to a solitary whale spending its day in the shallow waters, probably feeding… was this an omen that it would be a great day… but it honestly doesn't matter how many whales i see, for as long as i know i'm in their company, that's all that matters…. it was a beautiful day as we headed out towards Favorite Channel… my eyes were dancing across the waters trying to take all this in… memories of past trips kept slipping by only causing my anticipation to grow… at times i stood back and just watched the excitement of my companions… this might be their first time with the whales and these memories will be replayed countless times in their coming days… they will never get tired of telling of their time in the company of the whales…

and whales we saw… first an old friend came by to say hello and welcome me back…. when i saw its fluke, a smile came, for as Flame came back to Alaska, so did i… it was a beautiful welcoming as she arched her fluke up to the sky and let it come thundering down time after time… yes, i was glad to see her too… i could watch these whales all day… always waiting, searching the waters for their blow, and then endlessly hoping to see their fluke raised high as they make another deep dive… my thoughts drift to Rachel swimming with these gentle giants in the warm Hawaiian waters… she experiences a world i can't even imagine… what it would be like swimming in the deep blue waters and feeling the vibrations pounding through my being as the males sing their songs…

and to make this day even more special a pod of orcas graced the closing of our trip… today i stole even more memories for another time… it just felt good to be in their company again…

May 28, 2014

Whittier, Alaska

a beautiful cold, misty day with a light rain… the clouds are low over the mountains giving a grayish tone to my surroundings … i gaze at the forest… the trees are painted a beautiful deep green… Yes, it's a beautiful day… today i'll spend the day in the port of Whittier … at last a typical Alaskan day… this cruise, our first of the season has been met with sunshine in every port… sadly, i had to leave my XTRATUF, (Alaskans wear this brand of rain boots and they called them their sneakers… it seems Alaskans are born wearing them, marry with them on and finally get buried still wearing them)…

June 13, 2014

Southbound Glacier Bay, Alaska

worlds of ice and snow… a world formed thousands of years ago during the Wisconsin phase of the Pleistocene Ice Age… it's hard to comprehend that passage of time… a world totally void of life as we see today… life that no longer casts a shadow over this icy landscape… countless generations of life passing without being witnessed… evolution progressing ever so slowly, changing the life that walks these barren hills… today, in this dawn of time, the mountains are finally shedding their burden of ice and are now able to feel the warmth of the sun… the miracle of nature slowly painting these barren rocks with life… rocks that have been violently sculpted by the receding ice… moss and lichen giving way to the pioneer plants that yield to the shrubs and finally the trees of a forest… the succession of life… how many generations will slip by unnoticed as no one will be here to record this passing of time… i stand in the bitter cold with the wind blowing across my bearded face… my hat pulled down tight to keep the warmth from escaping… i stand and ponder this world of frozen solitude… the thunder of the caving ice… in this solitude i wonder what sounds are never heard…

i watch the black-leg kittiwakes as they fly about… they have journeyed with the winter winds over the oceans to find these blacken cliffs in which they will nest and from this another generation will fill these summers skies… i would love to steal their wings and fly into this frozen world… i wonder would i search for the same images that they seek… to fly over this river of ice and follow its tributaries to that distant icy kingdom that must rest over these barren peaks… a freezing wind blowing for an eternity yet is there anything to feel its chill in that empty frozen world…

for the past five days i have journeyed through this world of ice and snow… Glacier Bay to College Fjord… the grandeur of the glaciers of Prince William Sound… Harvard, Yale, Vassar and so many more all in a silent procession to the sea… then onward to Hubbard Glacier, the largest most impressive calving glacier in Alaska only to return to Muir's world of Glacier Bay… my eyes are still not tired of this beauty, this world of ice and snow…

i wonder, does this world even know of my travels to and from… one day i'm here and the next i'm gone… in reality i am but a dust of nothingness to this world that i leave behind yet my presence is felt in so many ways that i wish i was not a part… the carbon imprint of progress… what is the cost of our day of scenic cruising to this world that i love and leave behind?

June 16, 2014
Southbound Ketchikan, Alaska

a fishing story without any fish… the place was Ketchikan, the salmon capital of the world… as a matter of fact, it was the salmon industry that was lobbying for the Alaskan territory not to join the Union in 1959 as they were afraid of the federal controls that would be mandated on their fishing methods… salmon and fishermen are a big part of what makes Ketchikan, Ketchikan… heck, in the early 1900's when bordellos were found all up and down Creek Street in

Ketchikan, there was a saying "Creek Street was where not only all the salmon but also all the loggers and fishermen came to spawn"… now the King Salmon Derby has just ended in Ketchikan with the winner taking the $10,000 first prize with a fish weighing over 40 pounds… with this in mind, i know there are fish to be caught out there in the waters surrounding my little fishing town… so out i go on a party boat excursion with the hope of a King Salmon prize on my mind…

now i'm not a fisherman by any means… i don't own a fishing pole and can't even tie a fishermen's knot, but i love to fish, especially with my brother Jerry… i can spend days with him out in the bay catching flounder or whatever, and the fishing part of the trip really isn't that important, it's just the time we are spending together… but mind you, i have caught my share of fish during these trips even though my brother does a quick measurement and throws half of my catch back saying they're all "too small"… i never argue his decision but heck, i always think my fish is bigger than the one he catches and keeps… now, when it comes to surf fishing the story and my luck changes… for years i have fished the beaches of New Jersey with my brother and all i caught was every species of seagrass and seaweed that grows along the Jersey shore… my brother though will show me photos of striped bass that he caught on the very same beaches that are unbelievable… i swear there's a bait shop somewhere in South Jersey that has pet striped bass you can pose with….

now back to my fishing tale and Ketchikan… out we go on our party boat when i start to get the feeling that my fate probably isn't going to change… the last boat caught just one fish and it probably will not look any better for us… two then three hours drift by without even a bite… but i'm having fun chatting and listening to fishing stories… heck, i'm not even swatting green-head flies or mosquitoes, like back in New Jersey, so who's to complain… finally we get a strike… yea it's a King Salmon but wouldn't you know, it was too small… the fishing poles are set in rigging off the back off

the boat and as a strike occurs we take turns reeling in the fish… my turn will be last, so i'm hoping all the bait fish will have come and gone by the time it's my turn and i'll catch a keeper… another strike but it also is too small… no problem… then a big strike that yields a definite keeper in my eyes although it is a good stretch of the measurement that gets the required 28" necessary to keep the fish… one more then it's my turn and now the fish are starting to bite… but then i sadly hear "well its about time we head in"
so my luck of catching only broken promises in the ocean continues… but nevertheless i am a proud owner of a one day "Alaskan Fishing Permit"… i might just have to hang that on my wall as my trophy…

June 20, 2014
Northbound a week later in Ketchikan, Alaska
it began as a beautiful rainy day and to make things even better i was headed for Ketchikan again… don't ask me why, but out of all the ports we visit during the summer in Alaska, Ketchikan is my favorite and that's simply because Ketchikan gets the most rain… as we made our passage into Ketchikan my excitement for a beautiful rainy day was increasing by leaps and bounds… Deer Mountain, a 1200' peak overlooking Ketchikan, was lost in low clouds, and rain filled the air gifting me with a sea of puddles to splash through… yes i was in heaven… it was going to be a great day for a walk, yet my walk today would not be wandering through the streets of Ketchikan but instead a walk in an old growth red cedar forest…

usually i walk the Deer Mountain trail when i'm in Ketchikan, but today i decided to take an excursion out to a remote island in the Tongass National Forest north of town… in picking this excursion i found a hidden jewel, one that i'm sure i'll drift back to several times throughout the summer… our zodiac landed on a beach of weathered schist that sparkled from the waves parading in an endless rhythm onto the shoreline… the debris covering the beach was a treasure chest of pop-weed, bull kelp, black seaweed, ribbon seaweed, and sea lettuce… with my camera in hand i tried to find as many memories as i could on this beach… as i wandered aimlessly amongst my treasures, a light rain continued to fill the air… gradually we drifted into the forest to follow a boardwalk trail built by the forest service… this work of devotion was probably the labor of many hearty workers during countless rainy days just like today… it was along this wet wooden trail that the forest won my heart… i wandered amongst the giant red cedars with their fibrous yet reddish bark that kept calling for the touch of my hands… like a child i had to touch… crumble its scaly modified leaves in my hand… the scent of cedar… my head arched upward towards the falling rain to see the summits that formed the canopy of this forest… the endless sea of moss, ferns, and lichens formed a carpet that blanketed this world… so many times i wish i could have stopped and on my knees, like a child, let my hands wander through this world… and above this carpet the forest floor was filled with blueberries, false huckleberries, and alder shrubs… the guardians of this forest were the red cedars and mountain hemlocks that are found throughout the Tongass… many times i let myself fall back from this band of gypsies wandering among these ancient sentinels, wishing my boots would take me away from the crowds and into the solitude of this forest and finally losing myself in this world… i thought of many other walks that my boots have taken me on in the forest… the rainforest of the Olympics…. summer days on Admiralty Island… my memory chest is full of these treasures, and i only hope that there are more walks within these cathedrals in the future… it was a beautiful day and one filled with prayers of thanks…

June 21, 2014

Northbound Juneau, Alaska

it started with just a walk in the forest… the trees, they were the noble red cedars among which i spent several mornings ago walking among outside of Ketchikan… it seemed that the beauty and peace of the Tongass, and especially the trees that make this forest, would haunt me throughout this summer… but maybe haunt isn't the right word… the trees kept drawing me in, stealing my attention… yet i could never capture their images with my camera… the reflection of these trees within this forest are best kept frozen in my mind rather than in a single moment captured by a camera…

today in Juneau i hiked a trail that i meant to hike for many years… it seems that the whales always would draw me away, and therefore, the forest and this trail never got walked… but today, for some reason as i left the ship, Mt. Juneau seemed to be calling my boots to spend at least part of this day within its forest… so with several hours to idle away before the whales would once again capture my soul, i decided to walk out to the east of town, heading towards Mt. Juneau… soon my boots were leading me down a Juneau treasured secret, the Perseverance Trail… the Perseverance is actually a primitive mining road and not a typical trail that would be found within a forest of spruce and hemlock… the floor of this forest was carpeted with a thick layer of moss that was a bed for an abundance of wildflowers… my camera, time and time again, painted a canvas of all the flowers within this forest… i knew many flowers by their names from my countless walks over the years… at times the trail would open up with ragged cliffs of broken and weathered slate… its geologic story is one of weathering, burial, and folding or faulting… i still love to read the story told by the rocks… it's a story that is hidden from many without a geology background… secrets of its geologic history and age that are never to be spoken… and beyond the cliffs of slate a forest that stands far from my touch… i hesitated within this journey by a waterfall that i tried, time and again, to capture with my camera… was it the movement of the water rushing down or how its thunder filled my ears… still no luck…

i never made it to the end of the trail but i'm glad because now i know i must return again…as i began my hike homeward, the skies bathed the forest in a gentle rain… the canopy of this forest would shelter me from the rain but instead of seeking shelter often i stood and let the rain wash over me… it feels good to have the rain in my beard and run through my hair…

June 23, 2014
Northbound Glacier Bay, Alaska

during our sail today through Glacier Bay it was not the rivers of ice that captured my attention but instead the forest… the trees fading in and out of the low hanging clouds… the whispering of a mist playing hide and seek with these images… i chose the trees within these clouds to admire… reflections painted by their faded green silhouette against the mist… framing this canvas were peaks still dusted with snow from the winter that had silently passed…
i knew i was seeking images that others choose not to find… my camera was always searching, stealing images not of the glaciers but of the trees and the forest… trees and a forest that my boots will never walk… instead i captured these images for my soul to enjoy… it's always good to spend time in the forest…

June 24, 2014
Northbound College Fjord, Alaska

once again our journey takes us into a world of ice and snow… College Fjord will be our destination this evening and the sunny skies overhead do not look promising and so my "Alaskan liquid sunshine" will not cleanse my soul today… my task this evening, as we enter into College Fjord, will be to tell, to those that gather up on Deck 15, the geologic story of this fjord and the naming of the glaciers… even though i enjoy the sharing of this story, i find that it steals from my solitary moments, moments in which i escape alone into this world of ice and snow…

whether i'm standing on the open deck, among the passengers, or even narrating from the bridge with the officers of the watch, my talks are never taken from a script… i never really know exactly what i'm going to say… all the information, the facts and data, are there in my memory… i've given these talks for years now, so i really don't have to prepare… it seems the inspiration for what i will share simply comes from my heart… the heart of a naturalist… nature has inspired me all through my life… nature has been my spiritual voice…

once my obligations were over i wandered down to deck 7 where i was closer to the water… my perspective was more natural being there as i would look upward from the icy waters to the frozen world in the mountains… i found myself once again lost in the image of Yale Glacier… the late summer sunlight accentuated this world and stole my attention as i looked into an unknown world and followed that river of ice upward… the mountains with their winter dress of snow thrown upon them were dark and looked cold and forbidding… but it was those mountains, chiseled by the glacial gods through the eons that guided this river of ice on its journey to the sea… i tried to imagine the sound of the harsh winds, the stinging of the cold… it's a world that's unknown and where time really doesn't exist… the sounds from this world fall only upon empty ears… the concept of time changes… day and night still exist in this world but years and generations have no significance as this world has been here for an eternity and more…

i stood there lost in thought, for i know not how long… new thoughts now sadden my spirit… i wish it were not true but my heart knew that this world painted before me would never feel my boots upon its frozen skin… the reality of getting older… trying to accept my own mortality… as i turned to walk away i looked over at Harvard Glacier… i did not feel the need to stay, for i would return to this lost world of ice and snow again and again this summer… slowly walking away i suddenly felt a need to stop, i turned around, only for a moment to capture Harvard's image with my camera… i stole this image only to enjoy it in the days when my boots are far from Alaska… a prayer of thanks was whispered into this world…

The Story Behind the Name: College Fjord

During the 1890's Edward Harriman was one of the richest and most powerful men in the United States. Building his fortunes with the railroads, Harriman worked himself into poor health and was advised by his doctors to take a break from his work. Harriman decided to take his family on a maritime expedition to Alaska but later decided to turn this vacation into a scientific expedition. Like John D. Rockefeller and Andrew Carnegie, both well known for their philanthropic endeavors, Harriman turned his expedition into his own philanthropic effort by inviting over 50 of the top scientists of the day to join him on his Alaskan Expedition. Harriman would cover all costs.

Harriman hired Clinton Hart Merriam, the head of the Division of Economic Ornithology and Mammalogy at the United States Department of Agriculture, to head and recruit a team of scientists. Merriam was a graduate of Yale University with his doctorate from Columbia and at the time affiliated with Harvard University. Most of the scientists that Merriam recruited were also alumni or affiliated with Ivy League schools.

During this time it was very common for the captain of an expedition to name geographic features after sponsors of his expedition or a colleague he wished to honor. Prince William Sound was originally named Sandwich Sound by Captain Cook but later changed to Prince William Sound by Captain Vancouver in honor of Britain's Prince William. Within Prince William Sound the Harriman Expedition discovered a glacial fjord filled with many tidewater glaciers that had not previously been survey or explored. At the head of the fjord were two massive tidewater glaciers and Merriam is said to have named them both after the Ivy League schools he was affiliated with, Harvard and his alma mater, Yale. The glaciers on the starboard or right side as you proceed towards the head of the fjord were likewise named after the universities represented by many of the scientists. These schools, Amherst, Lafayette, and Columbia were all attended by men, while the schools on the left, or port side, were named after their sister schools such as Vassar, Smith, and Bryn Mar, all attended by women. Since the glaciers within this fjord were all named after colleges, the fjord became known as College Fjord.

June 27, 2014
Southbound Glacier Bay, Alaska

I once had a girl
Or should i say
She once had me

Lennon and McCartney

the introduction to this Beatle's song, Norwegian Wood, was played by George Harrison and marked the first time the sitar was heard in rock music… all night long this beautiful song ran through my head… it was like i had my very own Beatles concert playing in my head… so to you Giovanni, my dear friend who is the guitarist for the Princess Band on the Island Princess, i give my thanks for having the patience to show me how to play this song on my guitar… yes, the ballet your fingers danced across my guitar strings made my guitar gently sing… if only my hands could dance this same dance across the strings, so gracefully and effortlessly as your fingers seem to do… i ask myself, is it wrong to ask for this gift with all the gifts my boots have given to me…

i awoke this morning to sunshine and blue skies… because i haven't seen these skies in so many days i almost forgot what they were like… our passage this morning took us around Cape Spencer and as we were preparing to round the point of Cape Spencer, the sunlight bathed the snow covered peaks of the Fairweather Range in a beautiful alpine-glow… majestic monuments that were carved by the "Elder Gods" as John Burroughs once stated… i had to try to paint this image with my camera even though i knew my camera could never capture the full essence of this world created before me… the feelings i felt during those endless moments that i lingered in worship would be remember far longer than the frozen moment of time my camera tried to capture…

yes, we were heading once again towards Glacier Bay where my eyes would hopefully find refuge within the snow-covered peaks and the silent solitary rivers of ice… Brady Glacier was passed off our port side and i wondered how many eyes even saw this massive sea of ice or the blow of humpback whales in the far distance…. i smiled warmly thinking that this was just another typical Alaskan morning…

June 28, 2014

Southbound Skagway, Alaska

i have this old blue t-shirt that i bought over 25 years ago when i first came to Alaska… it's now an old faded shirt whose days have come and gone, but i still will wear this shirt to bed in the winter when it's cold… some things you can just never let go of… well the t-shirt shows a miner hiking a trail, the Chilkoot Trail… i always had that trail on my bucket list to hike one day…

the origin of that trail began long before the rush to get into the gold fields in the Klondike… this trail was probably first formed by wildlife as either a trail leading to a feeding area or a migration route across the mountains… the Tlingets then started using this as a trading route carrying eulachon grease, dried fish and other marine products in exchange for furs, clothing and other products from the interior. According to Parks Canada, "In 1880 the US Navy negotiated an agreement with the Tlingit to allow prospectors and exploration groups to make limited use of the Chilkoot Trail. Within short order it became established as the primary route by which prospectors made their way into the upper Yukon River basin."

well yesterday my boots finally took me down that trail… no, i didn't hike the 33 miles from Dyea up to Lake Bennet in Canada… and i didn't have to carry a hundred pound load strapped to my back… it was not in the dead of winter with the long steep climb up the Golden Stairway awaiting… neither did i have to put my load on the scales for the Canadian Mounties to record, only to return again with another load… but i walked the trail just the same…

well sort of... i was only able to hike just the first 3 miles into that journey... but as i walked i let myself linger off behind the others to try to steal a few moments in solitude... my boots carried me over the same trail that those stampeders hiked... their footprints have now disappeared from this trail and only are remembered in the memories lost in journals that were written long ago... i wonder, were they the ones who put the "trail blaze" in that tree... or was it from still a longer lost time when the Tlingits traded over these mountains... did they stop to pick the berries that today have not ripened yet for me to enjoy... was this rock, by the side of the trail, a place of momentary refuge from the endless hours of hiking... i wonder, what were their thoughts in those moments of rest... did they question their effort, for their backs and shoulders must have ached from the countless loads they carried... or did they just hike on until their feet could carry them no more... and of the bridges that i crossed... they had to ford these rivers in what could easily end up as a deadly encounter with the icy waters of the river... a river fed from the glaciers lost yet in another world... my walk was in a different time... but i walked still the same... was that shadow i felt behind me their ghost... a ghost telling me their broken stories...

June 30, 2014
Southbound Ketchikan, Alaska

names... we give them to so many things that we hold dear such as Joshua my golden retriever... it just wouldn't seem right to call Joshua after an inanimate object... sometimes names are bestowed on a geographic feature, as with College Fjord, because it will help us to recall or identify that feature...

some names, such as the name of a boat, will traditionally get passed on from one owner to the next... maritime tradition declares that it's bad luck to change the name of a boat until you pay respect to Neptune, the roman god of the ocean, asking for his permission... Tranquility is the perfect example of this maritime tradition… Tranquility is the name of a very special lady, my Catalina 30ft tall rig sailboat… i am the third proud guardian of this boat… her name has stayed the same now through all three owners… another maritime tradition i was taught by… my grandfather at a very young age was… that you always treat your boat as a lady and if you do that, your lady in return, will always take care of you… so in this moment of time am i the owner of Tranquility? i feel i can't say "owner" as it's Tranquility that possesses my soul, not the other way around… in the years since Tranquility floated into my world i displayed my love for my lady with my hands as they toiled so dearly over her soul… her brightwork or the varnished wood that dresses her so elegantly, always looks perfect… i know too that in future days to come there will be sadly other hands to caress her… i just hope who ever imagines that they possess her soul will still give her the honor of keeping her name…

well where is this all going and how does it all tie into my time here in Alaska… what you now read is a journal of my thoughts while i took a journey… mostly they are random thoughts brought on by a moment that i held on to dearly… these rambling thoughts though bear no name… and i know there are some things that we do not burden with a name… a kayaker will never name his kayak as he feels is just an extension of himself… you can never get closer to the sea and feel its spirit until you are in a kayak… being a part of that kayak you can feel the ebbing of tides as you paddle… you become one with the sea as you are the swells that roll gently to distant points…

well this gathering of words and thoughts that fill these pages are really nothing more than an extension of what i am, yet i feel they must bear a name… today i gave birth to its name: "Tidal Ebbings: A Naturalist's Reflection of an Alaskan Journey"…

July 7, 2014
Northbound Glacier Bay, Alaska
and a thank-you to a brother

this northbound journey became special to me as my brother Jeff cast his shadow along with mine… because of his presence, this journey of the past week held special memories for me… my brother shared in a world that many of my friends and even my siblings know not of… his boots walked with mine and shared in broken fragments of time that would be cast into the memories that he carried…. i saw his smile… his eyes excited with this image of Alaska that he was seeing… he now knows a special part of me, and my world, that so many others are not aware … the eagles and whales are now a part of his memory as they are mine and what is even more special is that i am a part of his memory…

often our lives pass silently by never knowing the world that the other walks in… it means a lot to me when a sibling takes the time to walk "in my dust"… and as i chatted with folks and told the stories of the glaciers and whales, i knew that he was seeing, first hand, the world that i walk in… we shared endless moments getting caught up in each other's joys… the world that is hidden because of the distance that is etched between us… at times it felt great just knowing he was here… that he took the time to see this world that i walk in…

the days are slipping by… northbound, southbound, hell at times it seems hard to keep track of where i'm heading… yet at other times i know it's always Wednesday as the passengers' suitcases line the halls the night before they must leave… and the following day is always greeted with sad farewells yet new hellos… so go my days… and as these days pass by, so do the many faces… at times i get confused associating the many faces with a particular journey… yet as all the different faces gather over the many journeys, they too all seem to become one… i wonder… does my face get lost within their memories… is my name a part of their memory of Alaska… i guess what really matters is that over this summer our paths did cross and because of that we both smiled and that moment became special… i think now of all those many faces, faces with names that are now lost in the winds of this summer… so many memories of smiles i hold…

i wrote this poem to a good friend when i was stationed in Greenland… his time was served and he was heading home only to be replaced by another face… in reading these words you can think of "carousel" as being life in general or simply this past cruise.. i realized this poem now speaks of the feeling that i face as each cruise ends and i say my goodbyes to friends i held dear in the week that passed…

a friend departs, Greenland 1975
farewell to a friend

the carousel has stopped.
the music is no longer heard,
one more rider disembarks for yet another ride,
and only his memory can bring back
all of the laughter…
it's in these quiet moments,
the waiting
for the carousel to begin again,
an empty silence,
waiting and wishing for our laughter to return
but it won't ever be the same again…
as our rider leaves,
we get a new face…
can he fill the empty shoes…
i hope not
for it would ruin a fond memory…
the carousel begins again.

jtalarico

and to the whales, i thank-you… if you could only see the excited eyes and hear the memories that were spoken because of you… i told them your story… the magic that you can cast… and now because of you, their souls were deeply touched and because of that your names will always be spoken as part of a special memory…

July 9, 2014
Southbound Whittier, Alaska

and so the cycle continues… i said good-bye to a brother today as our shadows will walk their separate paths till some future times… i often wonder why our laughter must fade with this distance, our smiles no longer held close… i beg to hear his laughter fill the air around me just one more time… Jeff's laughter is deep and fills the air around me with joy… i love the sound of the word "brother"… to me it's a symbol of a special bond… this time together with Jeff was good, making it harder not to hear the sound of his voice… life is often filled with good-byes…

and i think of Joanne… i miss her so much today, her smile, her scent, the sound of her voice… and of course i miss Joshua… i wish we could take our morning walk today…

July 10, 2014
Southbound in the Gulf of Alaska

i walk the Promenade deck in the early hours of this new day… the ship's fog horn breaks a silence that the fog has bestowed upon us… the sea appears a sullen gray and the wind is asleep with the storm petrels resting quietly on the swells…

during the long winter months, in the Gulf of Alaska, storms and cloudy days are very common… a ship of sail traversing this world can go days and sometimes weeks without seeing the sun… in the days before satellite GPS, or even Loran, navigation at sea was done with a sextant taking a sighting on either the sun or stars, both which necessitate a clear horizon for an accurate reading… if the ship's navigator were unable to take a daily sighting with the sextant, the ship's position would not be known until sky conditions improved which could have been days or weeks away…

A Story from thePast

The Czar of Russia, Peter the Great, formed the Great Nordic Expedition that departed St. Petersburg in 1733… it was 10,000 strong with soldiers, carpenters, engineers and scientists orders from Peter the Great to map Siberia, build the city of Petropavlovsk and sail across the unexplored Bering Sea until they struck North America then contain due south to Mexico.

Eight years later during the second phase of the maritime expedition, the fleet had been winnowed down to two worm-riddled boats manned by a crew plagued by scurvy.

It was in 1741 that Alaska was actually first seen…, the expedition was being plagued with countless stormy seas and cloudy days assuring that Bering never really knew his exact position… week after week and storm after storm they fought their way through the sea hoping to see some sign of land… the ship's naturalist, Georg Steller, paced the storm-washed wooden decks, keeping a watchful eye into the clouds hoping to spot land… then only for a second or two his eyes fell upon the image of a mountain… that image was not seen again for several days due to the continuing bad weather… but when it was sighted again, by the captain of the St. Peter, they knew that the New World was in sight and their journey of hardship would soon reap its reward… the captain, Bearing, named the mountain, St. Elias, after the patron saint of the day… no one knew that this event would mark the dawn of Russian Alaska.

and in reminiscent to that day our ship, the Island Princess, was once again lost in a world of thick clouds… our voyage today was marked not by the blue cloudless skies of yesterday but by the haunting sound of our ship's horn… again and again the fog horn sounded out our passage through these waters… our world today was a canvas of grays painted with a sky without horizons… our journey seemed to be at a stand-still in this world of gray… one had nothing to mark our passage, as our passage seemed to blend with the mist and fog swallowing us into this silent world… the ship's horn sounded again…

July 14, 2014
Ketchikan, Alaska

i can't think about Alaska without thinking about the "B" word… no it's not "bears" although without a doubt, it's bears that are on everybody's mind… no, for me its "boats"… and when you say "boats", it's the port of Ketchikan that paints a wet and salty canvas on my mind… i think i first fell in love with the port of Ketchikan on our very first cruise to Alaska… i still remember standing watch on the rainy deck as we made our approach to this port… the rain felt good as it washed the dust of the desert from my soul… but at the end of the day it was Ketchikan's fishing boats that stole my heart…i still have that image of the "Northwind" making her way to port… her sweat, salty and crusty painted her decks, and upon those who live on the sea… what stories her sweat could tell…

at the south end of town, just off of Creek Street, rests Ketchikan's fishing harbor… a strange silence falls over this harbor… many of the boats are anchored in a solitary peace knowing their work on the sea is in the past… yet some boats are enjoying the last minutes of this now broken peace as they must soon head out into an unknown sea with its face always changing with the wind… at times the wind will whistle in her rigging as you plow homeward, tired and wet… your hands trying to steal warmth at every opportunity… your life is hard… i know not of your joys or frustrations, and i can't even imagine the many faces of the sea that are part of your memories… your pain… muscles that ache and dreams of a warm and well deserved rest which is the reward of this part of your world… i long to listen to the stories your hands can weave… they are honest hands… calloused and harden from your world… and of your face, there is a beacon that shines from your eyes when the sea is mentioned… it stole your heart many summers ago… you have no choice but to return time and time again to the chorus of gulls with the wind in your face… the sea will never release your soul…

July 16, 2014

Northbound Vancouver, B.C.

my journey has now been over two months long… the rituals of my passing days have found a rhythm with the tides… i still hear Joanne's voice, though, often in random phone conversations… it reminds me of the world i left behind… my world now seems to be fragmented, held together by new memories, faces and voices that filled my days over the distant miles i voyaged this summer… but my shadow, faithful Joshua, i so deeply miss him… i miss his scent on my hands, his presence always so close to mine… a toy brought to me with the hope of a game of fetch… Joanne understands my absence and she will soon be reunited with my soul… our hands can once again hold our most treasured possession, that of each other… but of Joshua, he knows not nor understands why his best friend has left… does he long to hear my voice and smell my scent… many days must fade away before we can walk side by side again…

today in Vancouver the sun shone brightly, its warmth felt good as a few of my shipmates joined me to pass the hours walking the streets of the city of Vancouver… we drifted down to the water and wandered towards Stanley Park… my eyes were held captive by tall masts sitting silently in the harbor with sails waiting patiently to be filled with the wind… images of a sailboat from just yesterday, its sails reefed down, the ocean spray cleansing her spirit… she danced into the gusty winds, alone and free… her image painted again and again in my memory… she was northbound… i watched her for what seemed like an eternity… i thought of my lady Tranquility, waiting patiently in her berth for my hands to take her once again into the awaiting winds… our spirits free and dancing in the breeze of summer… and as evening came once again i watched the passing image of Point Atkinson Lighthouse off our starboard side… another journey northward beginning …

July 17, 2014
Northbound out of Vancouver, B.C.

i woke this morning to blue skies scattered with patches of pillow-like clouds… we were heading northbound leaving the protected waters of Queen Charlotte Strait behind and already i could feel a definite chill in the wind… entering the waters of Queen Charlotte Sound, the rhythm of the swells from distant points rocked our boat letting everyone know we were once again heading for blue water… even though Canada's Graham Island lies far to our west, my horizons will seem endless today… the cries of the gulls will fade as my world becomes one of shearwaters and petrels… i will search for my albatross dancing freely in the ocean winds, wandering on a journey like mine… its soul also held captive by this ocean…

July 19, 2014
Northbound, Juneau, Alaska

and to the whales-once again i was in your company… it always feels good to know that you are near… i listened to the excitement of the voices of those who came to spend time in your company… you did not disappoint their soul… i love to see your blow, glistening in the sunlight… its sound fills the air and my soul with joy… i watch your broken-back as you raised your fluke high to the heavens and then dove only to leave me alone to wait patiently for your blow to return… it's funny, i wonder how i can be among so many voices and yet be captured and lost in my thoughts, alone but within this crowd…

July 20, 2014
Skagway, Alaska

today i am planning to do nothing… i've already been to the gym, as my daily routine has me there every morning at 6:00 a.m. unless i need to be on the bridge doing a narration... my boots lie scattered across my cabin floor from my hike yesterday afternoon... today i want to put my thoughts from the past few days to paper, preserve them for days to come when i want to drift through those faded memories...

this summer my heart has been stolen again and again by the clouds... a peaceful drifting mist... whispers of solitudes... their faces slowly changing with the gentle stirring of the wind... the trees, their silhouettes fading in and out as a silent fog slips through this world that i stand within... i fear that if i wander from this canvas my soul will regret what i will never know... often i stood in the cold, but it didn't matter, for it was a small price my spirit paid for those solitary moments...

the past few days i spent reading an old friend... one that i first read many years ago and it feels good to hold this friend once again... i love the feel of a book in my hands... each book has its own feel... pages aging with time... folded corners or notes scribbled on pages, memories left from another time...

Aldo Leopold's *A Sand Country Almanac* was my companion this past week... thoughts of a brother always come to my mind with this book... this book speaks of the passing of the seasons as seen in nature and my brother follows the passing of the seasons using the birds... he has watched the migrations of the ducks from his beloved salt marshes since his youth... i envy his memories... moments that were probably silently witnessed while finding his shadow as his only companion... i love to walk by his side, in his world... to touch but for a moment his joys... i worry that our time together is short... the distance between us is too great... quiet moments of standing side by side when the need not to talk is more important than the words that would be said...

my seasons have change also... from my patio back in Sun City West, Arizona, i do not witness any migrations... my quail, mourning doves and finches are constant... i often wonder why i do not take the time more often to walk the desert... i remember fondly the years spent doing my desert tortoise research in the Maricopa Mountains about 50 miles southwest of the Phoenix area... during those years i watched the passing of the seasons from the wildflowers that would fill my desert basins, the blooming of the palo verde, mesquite trees, saguaro cacti, the summer grasses that replaced the wildflowers... yes, the desert has its season and holds a special place in my heart... my soul is tortured in all that i want to do... my boots are always there for me, waiting... they have been patient... a good friend that i can count on always to be there waiting...

a story about boots

it's funny but there are some things that i just cannot stand to part with... most of us have a garage as part of our house that was designed to keep the car in... well with time there seems to be less and less place for our car as we accumulate those fragments of past days that we just can't find the strength to part with... and in my garage there is a closet that i hold sacred for in that closet are all my old hiking boots... none of these boots can be worn again as they all show the marks of time that i have walked with them over countless trails... i can look at a pair of boots and know the year and the trails that we walked... how do you part with a friend like that... you can't, so the closet slowly got filled over the years...

written for some very special friends
this pair of boots
worn and soiled
but cared for
walked with
when i chose only my shadow for my company

and this pair of boots
with your tired touch
you showed me the desert solitude
mountain highs
we walked in the quiet rain
you helped me through the winter's snow
fields of wildflowers
canyons of rocks

and this pair of boots
we walked along country roads
been drenched by the desert sun
you carried me through the miles
quiet, deserted trails
a rock by a river's bank

and this pair of boots
you sat silently amongst my circle of friends
we passed a bottle
a warm, Indian fire burning
the laughter
you my friend, were a witness to my smiles

and it's always my boots
when the day is late
and the sun sinks low
and the mountain's solitude turns to a faded, grayish
blue
against a tired evening sky
it's always my pair of boots
that will carry me home to you my love

jtalarico
written sometime in the mid 1970's

July 21, 2014

Northbound Glacier Bay, Alaska

another passage will soon come to its end, but for me this journey continues… yesterday once again was spent in the shadow of Glacier Bay… we were met with blue skies and a horizon that revealed the mountain peaks that are so often hidden… i contemplated this canvas before me… who am i to judge its beauty or should i say its many different moods… as i walk the crowded decks, lost in my own solitude, i find that my spirit misses the clouds, the fog and the rain… this image painted before me is all too bright… the sunlight painted the glaciers in a white-wash that erased the multitude of blues that gave this wall of ice its texture, its life… that pallet of blues, painting the glaciers, would always cause my eyes to dance from image to image… the glaciers would just seem to be more alive… but today the blues have faded, yet the gull's cries still fill the air

and of today my thoughts are of her, on her journey… Joanne will join me in Whittier and once again our hands will join and her name will be heard often… but of my favorite shadow, my Joshua, he will wait patiently alone… is his heart broken and sadden that i stole her from him… i long for his companionship, to hear my voice echo his name throughout our house… to feel the unconditional love of a dog… i miss you, Joshua…

July 22, 2014

Southbound Gulf of Alaska

so often during this summer, low clouds and curtains of mist weaved a haunting shadow and colored my world various shades of gray… islands faded in and out…. trees, stood guardian over these islands and slipped from my view as the fog silently danced through the summer… the cold and dampness wrapped around my body as i stood on the wet decks and looked out on the gray forbidden waters…

it's strange but my soul prefers these days… my black woolen cap protects me from the mist… with the eyes of my father, i try see the images that his eyes would see… my eyes drift and wander without any given purpose… the sea has possession of my soul, i feel it was stolen from me many years ago… my love for the sea is a gift from my mother… did the sea steal her soul also as a youth… today i missed the cry of the gulls…

July 28, 2014

Southbound Ketchikan, Alaska

like a broken dream this journey continues to fade in and out just like the misty clouds that have followed me through this summer… today i sit looking out a window at the rain… it's been raining throughout the day and i'm in my beloved Ketchikan without anything that needs to be done… my rain-boots lay in silence missing my feet walking carelessly through the puddles like a child… the warmth of this room feels good… still a part of me aches to wander in this rain, to cleanse my soul, but instead i sit with Joanne silently reading… napping if we see fit… i glance often at her image… it feels good to hear my voice say her name out loud again… still my heart knows only too well that something is missing… my heart longs for his empty shadow by my feet… i miss you Joshua…

i reflect back to yesterday, i was in Juneau with Michael Ho, a brilliant wildlife photographer and dear friend, and his wife… it felt good to hear their voices and for us to walk side by side again… sharing many of our journeys in our walk… i love to see the sparkle in his eyes as he recalls the many memories that he paints with his camera… it's because of him that my images, painted with my camera, have come to be… like a parent he patiently teaches me his secrets… secrets that he has mastered to a perfection… the images on his canvas are never those that paint my canvases…

the whales were the reason why we shared this day together… i always love to feel and hear his excitement as his camera fires, burst after burst… i wonder what reflections his eyes see and why they are different from mine… we both are absorbed in this world created by our cameras… painting memories and always stealing moments in time for an eternity…

and what i remembered most of those moments is the trumpeting of the whales and how that sound filled my soul… their broken backs arched… flukes disappearing into a unknown world… we watched them bubble-net feed time and time again always…

watching the gulls and trying to solve the mystery of where and when my whales would surface to my world… yet our time was limited and soon came to its end…

we parted that day knowing we would eventually walk together again… smiles would be etched on our faces as we would recall our different journeys… there is a bond forged between us by our cameras… the camera's ability to steal isolated moments from a past only, so we can carry those moments with us forever in our memories…

thank you, Michael and Val for the friendship…

August 5, 2014
Northbound College Fjord, Alaska

sunshine and blues skies followed us every day as we sailed northbound… i missed my rain though and the chill in the air that it brings… but with the calmer seas and blue skies, the passengers walked the decks and searched for whales… and their prayers were answered as whale sightings were numerous throughout our voyage… spotting any type of marine wildlife always brings a thrill to the passengers… i love how they will seek me out to share their joy of a whale sighting especially anytime orcas are seen… it makes me feel so good that they have this need to share their joy with me… i always hope and try to make my presence on this ship as a positive experience for them… i feel i am here solely to enhance their journey with my stories that i weave while sitting on my stool in the Princess Theater…

around 8 a.m. i made my way up to the bridge to give a brief narration… i chatted briefly with the officers of the watch and got an update on our weather for later today when we would enter

Prince William Sound and eventually College Fjord… i came up to the bridge to comment on the island far off our starboard side… the island is named Kayak Island and is easily identified due to its profile which appears as that of an old fashion key… it was on this island that Russian feet first set foot in the New World… George Stellar was the the naturalist for Bering's maritime expedition and was only on this island for three hours, but within that time he was able to confirm that this was truly the New World and not a part of Peter the Great's kingdom… it seemed that Stellar was an avid birder and knew just about every bird within the eastern borders of Russia… when Stellar was a student in Moscow, he viewed an image of a bird that he would never see in any part of Russia… the bird was a bluejay and was found in one of the new colonies in the New World… Stellar was only on Kayak Island for a short period of time when he spotted a bluejay… today that bird is known as a Stellar BlueJay and was evidence to Stellar that this truly was the New World…

as i have in each of our journeys through College Fjord, i told the story of the glaciers to those ears that yearned to understand all that surrounded us… yet still, even after so many journeys through this fjord, i always find time to stand in my own solitude and whisper a prayer of praise for how this story unfolded…at times i find that i just can't get enough of Alaska… i was getting ready to share a late dinner with Joanne and a very good friend of ours, it would be the last dinner we shared together for a while…

i knew i would not be able to say grace with Joanne again or see her reflection for far too many dinners, yet my eyes were drawn time and time again to this world of ice and snow just outside our window… with my camera in hand, i asked her, with my eyes, if just for one more time i could try to capture the magic that surrounded us… i begged a promised of a quick return as i hurried away… i can look at these glaciers week after week, and i always see them just a little different… it may be the fog, a light rain, the scattering of clouds, the angle of the sun's rays or simply my mood, but this canvas always is painted just a little different… i aim my camera seeking just the right composition for what my heart feels…frame after frame my camera records the light forming images… but then can you really capture the essence of that moment with a simple exposure lasting only a fraction of a second?

August 6, 2014

Southbound Whittier, Alaska

a major part of my world has slipped away from me today and my heart aches with good-byes… Joanne boarded her bus this morning and is headed home… life is so full of good-byes… it's a cloudy and rainy day today, simply a reflection of my spirits, but in my heart i know there are many sunny days over my horizons… it's just the journey to those horizons that are sometimes full of heartaches… my mind drifts through memories of Joanne and the past two weeks as they will be a treasure chest that i will carry and cherish until i no longer need to carry them… some memories in life you can let fade away while others you hold on to for a lifetime…. memories of her and the moments we spent together will sustain me until i hold her in my arms once again… and in these solitary moments i miss hearing her say my name and her name being whispered from my lips… i sit alone…. i feel the loneliness all around me, smothering any joy i have for this day… today i will read, nap, and play my guitar, but my heart and thoughts will be with her that i miss…

the dawn of yet another journey begins…

August 7, 2014

Southbound Hubbard Glacier, Alaska

the days are passing by, at times slowly like the ebbing and flooding of the tides… neap and spring tides will mark the months as i drift through my summer…

my thoughts return to our visit to Hubbard Glacier… it was just one of many visits throughout this summer, but this momentary pause in time i will remember for a long time… by the afternoon our clear skies had turned to low clouds and a light rain as we were being influenced by an approaching low pressure system that usually brings cloudy skies, rain, and even stormy seas… i reported up to the ship's bridge for my narration on Hubbard Glacier and chatted with the Captain and the Pilot regarding the Captain's intentions while visiting Hubbard Glacier… many people are under the assumption that the Captain is always steering his ship even though he may be doing it through his senior officers, but anytime we are in Alaskan coastal waters, an Alaskan pilot boards the ship to assist in the ship's navigation… the pilot is more familiar than the Captain with local marine conditions such as tides and currents while the Captain knows how his ship responds to these marine situations… therefore an interesting dialogue is always occurring between them or the Senior Officer of the Watch… even though it will be the pilot who is giving the headings to the helmsman, and not the senior officer of the watch, there is always a prior discussion between these individuals determining the ship's safest course… although it appears the pilot is now in full control of the ship, the Senior Officer of the Watch is always carefully listening to each of these headings given by the pilot…

after talking with the officers for a while, i go to my spot on the bridge for my narration… i usually stand off to the side, usually near the port wing of the bridge, with only my thoughts… looking out the huge windows, protected from the cold and damp rains i tell the story of the glaciers… i talk about this world of ice and snow and of a time when in its youth this river of ice stole all the mountains and forest and hid them forever from the sun and buried them deep within its soul…

Yakutat Bay, the entrance to Hubbard Glacier, is now behind us… sailing slowly inward and passing Haenke Island on our starboard side, allows us to slip cautiously deep within Disenchantment Bay, creeping silently into this world of ice and snow… staring upward towards that wall of ice, it is hard to comprehend its actual height… explaining to the passengers that what stands before them is more than twice as tall as our ship and taller than the towers of the Golden Gate Bridge in San Francisco puts this wall of ice into better perspective… walking outside the bridge onto a small navigational deck i am able to see the colors of the ice better enabling me to capture its true color… i stand there in silence and then suddenly the stillness breaks… i am hearing, as i have never heard it before, Hubbard's "white thunder"… a massive calving or breaking of the wall of the glacier is taking place… trying endlessly with my camera, taking burst after burst of images, but realizing it useless to try to capture something of this magnitude… putting my camera down, after the calving stops, my eyes follow tributaries that are flowing from this massive river of ice and journeying upward to the mountains that are hidden by the drifting clouds… i wonder how many lifetimes it will take my boots to discover this hidden world of ice and snow…

August 8, 2014
Southbound Glacier Bay, Alaska

and of Glacier Bay… i wonder have i grown tired of this journey… often i can now sit and read or pass quiet moments with my guitar and a friend… but deep within my soul i know i could never grow tired of this bay… i could never ignore that restless urging within me… i look out a window only to find myself putting on my shoes and jacket, my camera in my hand as once again i stand with the others and admire its beauty… my camera has captured its image so many times, but still i find it's impossible to capture its being… often i lose myself in the clouds, for without the clouds the mood of this canvas feels empty…

August 9, 2014
Southbound Skagway, Alaska

we are standing by the river feeding into Lutak Inlet, the rain falling intermittently but steadily enough to wet the ground i stand upon… i do not care if i am getting wet, hell it feels like i've been wet most of the summer... a brown bear is feeding by the river on the abundance of Sock-eye salmon... this is the last salmon run of the season and maybe this mama bear's last chance to build her fat reserve for the long winter that will soon come...

a multitude of cameras... frame after frame the cameras shoot while each of us tries to strategically position ourselves... i don't know when i realize that something is...

wrong with this picture... is this really the wilderness that i am striving to capture and be a part of, or is this nothing but a tourist attraction with a bear as the main draw... slowly i lower my camera and leave...

August 12, 2014

Southbound, one day out of Vancouver, B.C. journeys are often comprised of good-byes, and my heart has learned that the goodbyes are the painful or bittersweet part of any journey... some journeys are so overpowered by goodbyes that it's all we remember of that passage of time... one cannot find the reward of the journey, for the sting of the good-bye is so harsh... this part of my journey is now full of the bittersweet, but i must believe in tomorrow, in the sunrise that will always come, and let this pain slowly drift away as with the ebbing of the tide...

working on a cruise ship as a naturalist puts me into two different worlds.... in one world i am a passenger with all their accommodations, a private cabin and eating in a variety of dining rooms... in the other world i am a crew member... this world i have come to enjoy and feel proud that the crew considers me one of their ship mates... it's in this world that i have met some of the most genuine people... people whose laughter and smiles i hope i never forget... upon boarding a new ship, the first thing i always do is to seek out those long lost smiles, smiles upon which over the years are many... now the bitter-sweet...

to my friend Rex, the officer in charge of all the ship's excursions.... you have blessed my world with your presence... for two summers now i have enjoyed hearing the sound of your name from my lips… seeing your beautiful smile and hearing the laughter that you filled my world with… memories of popcorn, a glass of wine or dropping in your office to say a hello and above all, your unselfish generosity… the many memories my camera has captured would not have been possible if not for you… i am so happy that you are finally able to go home as you look so tired my friend… am i being selfish though in saying i hate to see you depart… i must believe that we shall laugh together again…

and to all those faces that have graced my time on these seas, i hope you remember me as i remember you… i pray that your laughter never fades, and i thank you all for your friendship

i am so blessed by being a part of these two worlds and so, as if on eagles' wings, i sail on…

17 August 2014

Northbound Skagway, Alaska

a happy birthday to my brother, Jeff… i always remember that you and Davy Crocket were born on the same day…

my days continue to drift by as the carousel of faces continue to pass… the pain i feel because of those who left slowly ebbs as my patterns and habits continue to carry me along…

i think back to the book, *A Sand Country Almanac,* and i too notice the passing of the summer from the flowers that color my world… it was late in spring when i arrived with the skunk cabbage all in bloom… i can remember those early summer days when snow was still to be found high in the mountains of my beloved Ketchikan… summer was just around the corner as told by the color blooms … blooms that graced the trail i walked still buried in the deep snow of a winter that was trying to slip away… actually the metabolic activity of the skunk cabbage is so great that the plant's new growth will melt the frozen world it lives within, allowing the bloom to rise above the drifts formed from the winter's snows… then with the approaching summer all my berry bushes will begin to flower so that i can eventually feast on my salmonberries and blueberries… as summer continues to unfold, the roadside will be carpeted by the purple flowers of the fireweed… then as summer closes, the berries fade and the fireweed turns to cotton telling me once again that summer will end and my journey will soon be over… the bears will begin to feed on the late salmon run in the Chilkoot and with this the cycles of migrations scream out to me that the final days of my summer are nearing… i even noticed today a different chill in the air… soon the first snows, or as they say in Alaska, termination dust will paint the mountain tops… yes, this calendar of nature speaks volumes to me…

my time spent in our ports now has no sense of urgency… i am content to just know that i am here… my boots can now rest quietly as i find comfort in my world of books… my guitar has felt my fingers throughout this journey as i continue my struggle to let its music fill my soul… thanks to a very special and talented friend who had the patience during this voyage to teach my fingers to slowly dance the ballet that causes my guitar to sing… i love to watch his fingers so graceful and silent as they release my guitar to cry the blues or fill my soul with songs that have carried me through my journey of life…

the books that have been read now fill a part of my book shelf… their pages have been turned slowly and filled my days with images, thoughts and new information of this world i journey in…

hopefully soon i will hold her again in my arms and see Joshua's shadow by my side… but for now my journey must still continue…

August 22, 2014
Southbound Glacier Bay, Alaska
there are a multitude of special places within this world we walk… each and every one of us who takes the time to let the earth feel our boots and let the wind blow freely through our hair will have a place that we feel is special… i've been blessed to have my boots take my shadow to many places that i hold dear, and here in Alaska it's really

no different… there are so many trails that i've hiked over the years and so many more awaiting my boots… but now things are different… they are different because i spend my summers on a cruise ship… no longer can i hike the divide trails of mountains, old growth forests trails, or kayak endless back-bays, coastlines, or lakes… because i spend my summers on a cruise ship, i must now take a passive role in experiencing this wilderness… my boots cannot wear the dust of the trail but must sit idly waiting for their friend to take them out to feel the earth… i take comfort in having the imagination of a child with the eyes of my father… my father would look at something and then let his imagination run wild interpreting what he saw… for in my mind i can walk away from this world i am confined to and dance in my dreams in this wilderness that surrounds me… and if during this summer i could have worn the boots of John Muir, i would have let them take me into that world of ice and snow in College Fjord… many voices speak of the beauty of Glacier Bay, but my spirit yearns for my garden within College Fjord… today i walked the decks and gazed into the beauty of Glacier Bay, but my vision is hungry for yet another destination, and all i admire today is always compared to my garden in College Fjord… i realize the ugliness of my reality… a reality that speaks a truth that rips my heart apart… my boots will never ramble through that world and my spirit will never feel how fragile it would be in that solitude… i wonder what sounds are carried in the wind that voyages through that deserted wilderness… through a place that has never experienced a footprint… does time really exist in that frozen garden.…

my books have taken me into many locations that my boots have not been able to take me to, yet i have never read the words that would let me know the soul of that world that lies beyond my grasp in College Fjord… so i must just use "my father's eyes" and stand in the solitude of my thoughts and imagine…

August 24, 2014
Southbound Juneau, Alaska

written to Rachel Cartwright, my friend, marine biologist and
author of the *Alaska Cruise Companion*

i went whale watching for what i figured would be the last time this summer as there is some hiking i still want to do… today my time with the whales was full of sadness as i really felt there were just too many boats on the water whale watching… mostly it's the smaller boats that feel they can get closer to the whales that bother me the most… i'm troubled and feel i must do something…

next summer (if i'm up here) i want to try to document what i'm seeing week after week… data that probably nobody is taking because it's data that may take dollars out of pockets of the industries that prey on the tourist's dollar… i want to chat with you to find if i am too far off base or if i have something that maybe be useful…

chat with you soon (check my blog for the photos i posted with this entry… i won't post anymore whale photos until i can feel right about what i'm a part of)…

jules

Ode to the Whales

it was a gray, cloudy day as the rain fell lightly making me think these rains were my tears of goodbye, i know not… today i determined it would be my last time to journey with the whales this summer… no longer would i be in their company, waiting patiently for them to grace this window of the sea that i sail upon, from now on i will only share but a minute in their company as we sail onward… too far to hear their blow, too far to reach into their world… today, as always, my camera hung by my side, yet i chose only to paint my pictures in my memory… the whales were few compared to many of the times we spent in each other's company this summer… now this summer is slowly fading to its end… soon their winter's journey will begin again as this carousel of time will speak to them…

but today my thoughts were so different as currently i'm reading a book, *The Dominion of Bears*... the bear, other than the wolf, is probably to many the last remaining symbol of our vanishing wilderness... we all try to take a piece of this wilderness for our own use, and in the end, we are just treading too heavily upon the bear's world, and they are forced to adapt... many cannot adapt and must pay the fatal consequence... are these gentle giants of the sea a symbol also of a wilderness we know as the ocean... a wilderness that we are slowly stealing away from those that need it... today i couldn't help feeling that we are loving these whales too much... i'm troubled also because i also journeyed to be in their company all summer long... am i too a part of the problem? i question, are there just too many of us (boats)... today i watched two whales traveling slowly by the shoreline ... were they feeding or just passing through, yet in their wake were six boats... were we chasing, watching, or disrupting, it's open to opinion... the whales though had but only one choice and that was to swim onward for they were surrounded on three sides by we who want to be in their company... too many times this summer i felt like this... did i speak out, no my camera was in hand wanting that perfect shot... and sadly against what i now question, always wanting to be but a little closer, maybe at a better angle for my photo... how wrong i was...

can i now just walk away not wanting to be a part of this picture... let my camera sit idle... and what of all those whose smiles and excited eyes i will never forget... did i not hold their hands and help them experience these whales for the first time in their lives... to spend but a minute in the company of these whales, a minute that will last a lifetime in their memories...

so for now i will bid my farewell... are these photos the last that i will try to steal... are they enough to last me my lifetime... my soul will cry if i choose to let you be free... but i feel i must...

August 28, 2014

Northbound heading to Ketchikan, Alaska

it has been a few days since the parade of new faces have become my surroundings… and with the new faces i must accept that there are many memories from my past journeys that i will see no more… to my friends with whom i shared so many moments, laughs, and friendships, you will always be missed… there are many times in life when people pass through our world and i question if it is our destiny that our paths crossed… for in these moments that we share, life's direction changes or is it just my focus on some aspect of life that seems to change… at times we flounder in this sea, drifting carelessly with the tides, our courses drifting as if our compass has been lost in a fog and our vision is obstructed… but then this person walks into our world, if only for a brief space of time, and once again our course is set as if the stars in the night sky become our guide…

with these thoughts in mind i cry to my friend, Giovanni (guitar player in the Princess Orchestra)…

if ever my hands could dance on the strings of my guitar and play all the songs that i've listened to, in those hours of solitude, where music has filled my soul… and of all those bluesmen, their names now faded in time, if my hands could only dance as their hands did across the strings, crying out the blues, my foot keeping time with the rhythm of my soul, the harsh sound of a slide across the strings singing the blues…

i love you my friend, for whenever i would say the name of a beloved song, you would always seem to smile, but for a second; then i would sit and watch as your fingers danced and the song's music filled my heart… yes, you drifted into my world and i chose to believe it wasn't by chance… without even knowing it, you directed my compass again… yes, i now have hope that with time my fingers will slowly learn that dance… my guitar still feels my fumbling fingers… i hold it on my lap often now as the hours float by… i chart this new course that you gave to me…

maybe someday in the future our paths will cross again, and if i am so fortunate, i promise that i will pick up my guitar and but for a minute show you the music in my soul, music that you gave to me…

August 29, 2014
Northbound Ketchikan, Alaska

the rain fell today… it wasn't a constant rain and at times it was just a drizzle… Deer Mountain was hidden in the mist, gray clouds drifting with the wind but never yielding my mountain… and with the rain there was a multitude of puddles awaiting my boots, yet the urge to wander today gave way to quiet time… a book in my lap, napping at times… there was no sense of urgency… i thought often of how in the desert we dream of a winter day like this, a good chill in the air, a hot mug of tea and slippers instead of boots for my journey, for slippers are for rainy days and day-dreaming… my music would play a faint symphony with the rain, and if i were at home, Joshua would lie at my feet and Joanne would be but a whisper away… but i am here and they are so far away…

i feasted on my favorite soup at lunch while the rains continued to wash this world that awaited my boots… and my boots could not resist this temptation and in the end i did take a short journey into this rainy world… it was a journey in search of my carved raven pendent that i hope would arrived from Haida Gwaii, an island off the coast of British Columbia, and owned by the Haida natives… yet as much as i enjoyed the solitude of my book, it felt good to splash through the puddles and feel the rain on my beard… my raven is still in flight for it hasn't arrived from the hands that carved my treasure, but i found a wolf on a copper wrist clasp that i will wear with my other raven… these are my amulets that keep the winds of Ketchikan always within my soul…

i did hurry back though to feel my guitar on my lap, my fingers trying to learn a new dance… and yes, my mug of tea…

as many came back from their wanderings, i heard excitement in the voices telling of their journey… they shared their time spent with bears… photos that will be looked at for many days to come… we chatted… tomorrow these passengers will be anxious to be in the company of the whales…

with the sounding of the ship's horn through the rainy mist, we left the port of Ketchikan behind us… today, in my lecture, i will talk of the whales that i love, and as i sit on my wooden stool, on the stage chatting, the passengers will always listen quietly… if only they knew the joy that they gave me, as i sit and weave my stories… my love of being in their company… being a silent part of their world for those precious moments that we share together… later in the night, when the rain no longer fell, we slowly slipped through Snow Passage and the whales came as i said and hoped they would… with excited eyes we all stood in our solitude and watched them bubble-net feed…

it was a beautiful day and i whisper my thanks…

September 5, 2014
Southbound Glacier Bay, Alaska
reflecting back over the last two days

it's been several days since we sailed southbound on yet another journey from Whittier… summer was still in the air as we were treated to blue skies and warm temperatures which was very unusual weather in Whittier, as it seems always to rain there… i once again let my boots wander on solid ground for the day without the gentle swells of the sea, the salt in the air, and the wind on my face… i colored my day in shades of green and brown with the scent of a tundra meadow… there was an abundance of berries on the bushes that soon found their way to my awaiting hands… i first headed over to Learnard Glacier to see if it was possible to approach this frozen and silent world… if i had the spirit of John Muir, i would have found a way up that talus slope, but instead, my boots took me to an old familiar friend (Portage Pass) where i sat on a saddle and let my thoughts drift carelessly as the image of yet another frozen silent world filled my soul…

it has been two days of a cold rain since we left our berth in Whittier… the sea, angry gray in color and alive as the swells continued to grow, spindrift filled the air while a lonely albatross danced its silent ballet through the maddening skies… the decks were constantly awash in this early winter storm, for summer had faded and winter showed its angry face… our southbound journey through the Gulf of Alaska…

the seasons are now in their rhythmic dance as the landscape is washed in new colors… the fireweed has turned to cotton and soon the new snows will dust the mountains… my reflection is painted to show the changing of the seasons… summer into fall, and fall into winter… i now wear my vest to keep me warm, and the wool of my cap feels good on my head while hot tea and hot chocolate are often found in my mug… i enjoyed this change of season as change is always good medicine for the soul…

today in Glacier Bay the clouds hung heavy and hid this world from my sight… a light rain could be felt throughout the day… the glaciers faded in and out of view at the will of these gray clouds while i still found myself on the decks, often alone in my thoughts… thoughts that now are of home… my feet have grown weary, and they yearn to take me to Joanne and Joshua once again… i want to hold her hand in mine, to see his shadow by my side…   my guitar is held often these days… it feels good in my hands and books are still held often, but my thoughts keep drifting to you my love…

September 6, 2014
Southbound Skagway, Alaska

i awoke to yet another gray day…the decks were wet from a recent rain and there was still a good deep chill in the air… i walked the upper decks in silence with the thoughts of the new day alive in my mind… soon i will talk to her whom i miss… i long to hear her voice again…

but as i quietly walked, dressed in the anticipation of hearing her voice again, i found what would cause me sadness throughout this day… alone on the empty deck and struggling in a silence i could not understand lay a small white-faced storm petrel… its right wing broken and no longer laying gracefully by its side… was it in pain as it lay there on the cold wet deck, i did not know… i gently picked this broken spirit up and held it tenderly in my hands… did it sense comfort in the warmth of my hands as i gently stroked the beauty of its feathers… as it cuddled in my hands, i could faintly feel the rhythm of its heart as it lay broken, silent in my grasp… with a wing that would no longer let it fly across the wild seas its fate was cast… the rules of nature can be harsh… death is a part of living, yet death is so final… i wanted to believe that this bird still had a spirit and time would heal its broken wing… let it feel the wind in its wings once again… i know better… and with much sadness in my heart i knew what i had to do and so i gently cast this soul into the dying winds and watched as it fell helplessly to the sea… and as i walked away in sadness i knew these moments would linger with me throughout this cold and gray day…

normally in Skagway i would head down to Haines, the Chilkoot River, in search of bears, yet on my last journey there, standing amongst many and watching a bear feed, i felt that i was no longer in a wilderness that feeds my soul.… this was not how i want to remember these bears… was it the fault of that bear, i think not, but instead the fault of being in the company of so many… today i choose not to walk in the shadows of so many… so to my bears i bid you farewell at least for this year… i don't want to love you to death, so instead i choose just to sit alone in thought and love the images that you granted to me through the years…

September 15, 2014
Northbound Glacier Bay, Alaska

it's been many days since i last sat and put my thoughts down… i am weary now… my boots are yearning to carry me home and thoughts of home are always on my mind… wanting to have her beside me, to do those little things that mean so much to the both of us…. to have someone to whom i can say "i love you"… and to have his shadow always being there, the unconditional love that one always feels from a dog… i must now try to find a balance with taking journeys and spending my time at home… this has been a long journey, a long time without them both by my side…

i walk often now without my camera in my hand… my eyes, have they grown tired? no, for i still see and feel the beauty in the passing moments, and i still frame and compose each view in my mind… looking for a composition that expresses the feeling or the mood of the moment, but now i never release the shutter to capture this moment for my hands are empty…

i sit often with my guitar… quiet time as i practice teaching my fingers to dance and fill the room with music… i regret that so many years ago i put my guitar down… the patterns my fingers played slowly faded and that music was lost… was it just frustration with my expectations or was it just the rhythm of my life changing as a new path was found to wander…

and of her that waits, Tranquility… i miss my time with that lady of mine, her smell, the salt air, the hours i spend in solitude caressing her and taking pride in her reflection… all those hours of messing around…

"There is nothing, absolutely nothing, half so much worth doing as simply messing around in boats"

Kenneth Grahame *Wind in the Willow* 1908

and of the wind… how my soul aches to feel the wind fill her sails, her bow dancing free and graceful through the water taking me away… yes i want to go home…

but as i stand in solitude and stare in silence at this world of ice and snow i say a prayer in silence… i pray to try always to live in the moment… life is too short to wish our time away… time will always pass and once that time passes it is lost forever…

yes, i think i will walk with my camera in my hand again today for there is always a picture that i haven't captured…

September 16, 2014
Northbound College Fjord, Alaska
often during many voyages one would find me in a shell of silence absorbed in one of many books that joined me on this journey… so what does a naturalist read to prepare for a summer sailing among the forest and glaciers and to gently pass the days of an Alaskan summer…

- *Where the Sea Breaks its Back* and *Steller's Island* as they both dealt with Georg Steller the German naturalist who joined Vitrus Bering on the first Russian Expedition to Alaska
- *White Planet* and *Secrets of the Ice* since one of the highlights of an Alaskan cruise are the glaciers
- *Mycophilia* for the fungi that i find in my solitary walks in the woods
- *Coming into the Country* by McPhee was a great reread on Alaska, one that i will always recommend to everyone
- *The Harriman Expedition* by Grinnell, *The Harriman Expedition Retraced,* and *Looking Far North: Harriman Expedition,* these books were read because College Fjord was named and studied by a group of scientists from the Harriman Expedition
- *The Whale and the Supercomputer* was an interesting book on the effects of climate change on the arctic ice and subsistence whaling by native Alaskans
- *Looking for Alaska,* a great book about Alaska, and the people that one would find traveling through all the corners of this state
- *Alaska Days with John Muir* written by the minister Samuel Hall Young who traveled with Muir up in Alaska

now when it came time to sort through my shelves of unread books in my library what would join me for this journey

Undaunted Courage… the Lewis & Clark Expedition… thank you to my sister Judy as it was a great read

Gifford Pinchot and the Making of Modern Environmentalism.... i took this book because of the Tongass National Forest that i would walk in throughout the summer

The Men Who United the United States

The Attacking Ocean: The Past, Present and Future of Rising Sea Level

The Harriman Expedition, the journal kept by John Burroughs

Sun Country Almanac, always a great read and causes me to think always of my brother Jerry

Dominion of Bears, the ecology and management of bears in Alaska

and for the music that always fills my soul:

Wild Tales by Graham Nash's

One Way Out: the Story of the Allman Brothers Band

Please Be With Me, Duane Allman's story told beautifully by his daughter

so my journey will continue as will the books that enrich my soul.... so to you mother, i thank you for all the walks we took to the library as a child and for the gift of reading that you encouraged in me

September 17, 2014

Southbound Whittier, Alaska

and the rain continues to fall... the sky is crying... it's been screaming all day long, so today i found comfort in the warmth of the ship.... my book was held often as the pages were slowly turned, and my guitar often felt my fingers learning the rhythm of a new song... a warm mug of tea was a constant companion to this rainy day... turnaround day (the day the old passengers leave and the new passengers arrive)... i choose to let my boots stay dry and not wander even though this will be our last time in Whittier for the season.... i know not when i'll return, but i'll always remember the rain of Whittier... it probably will be a rough passage tonight and tomorrow in the gulf since we sit within a low pressure system that refuses to move on… late September storms in the Gulf of Alaska occur about every 5 days and they can bring large storm swells with them… yes, the sea will be alive on this southbound passage… my port-hole windows are covered and bolted shut as we have just been informed by the captain that we should expect high seas and wind in our passage across the gulf… we were also requested to secure all loose items in our cabins… i do sleep better with the rolling and pitching of a spirited sea…

the last few days of our final northbound cruise were filled with intermittent rain, and now i wonder was it just a precursor of the days ahead… i said my farewell to College Fjord as the rain fell and the clouds hung low over this frozen world of ice… it was fitting that it rained as i like to think that they were my tears of another goodbye… and i did stand in solitude with the rain falling, warm in my rain gear and boots while my camera rested silent in hand… i only hope i painted that last image of the glaciers in my memory for when i'll return i know not…

this will be our final "southbound voyage" for the season… i am finally homeward bound… this cruise will be filled with the bittersweet, leaving Alaska, friends, the forest that i walked within, my whales, and my beloved town of Ketchikan, yet i know that soon i'll hold her in my arms and Joshua will be my constant companion once again

September 18, 2014
Southbound Gulf of Alaska, Alaska

the sea is alive… one can easily feel the broken rhythm as our ship struggles steadily through this wild sea… i sat by a window where i often read in silence, my book resting quietly on my lap…. i was lost in thought, spellbound by the mountains of waves that broke around us… i sat contented just to watch this storm…

to my brother Jeffrey, how we love the the Beaufort Scale, an empirical measure that relates wind speed to observed conditions at sea or on land has the winds today rated Force 11 or Severe Storm, hell Jeffrey this is worst weather than a Gale… i laugh thinking at how Jeffrey and i would have struggled to walk the deck to feel the force of the wind and to hear the whistling of the winds in the rigging, the rain pounding against our face with thoughts from our passage to Cape Horn… the winds are reaching 60 knots now with swells easily at 20 or more feet, so it's a good healthy storm in the Gulf of Alaska… the sea is a landscape comprised of mountains of gray waves… our ship shudders and struggles onward with each wave we encounter… the howling wind blows off the top of the waves and fills the air with a relentless gray mist… i think of all those who live on this ocean, who harvest its wealth only to know so well the many faces this ocean can wear…

my mug of tea is warm and my feet are dry… i fear not the next wave, knowing that…

the waves are usually in sets of 7, with the seventh wave in the set usually the biggest… i silently try to keep track of the sets of waves looking for the one that will be the one most feared… i sit spellbound by the fury of this sea, yet in silence i whisper a prayer in thanks for this spirited sea…

and yes i'm southbound to you my love…

September 20, 2014
Southbound Glacier Bay, Alaska

i'm southbound and every day i'm getting just a little closer to home… after our last stormy day at sea, the winds have subsided, but still a light rain falls silently… the skies are painted with gray clouds hanging low over the mountains… i loved the rain and clouds that descended over the bay and created a mystical mood that sunshine can never provide… i felt this would be the perfect setting for my last trip through Glacier Bay… i will carry all these memories with me throughout this coming winter… my photos will always remind me of those beautiful days that passed in this bay…

my farewell today had moments that will last forever… we were at Johns Hopkins Glaciers, a glacier that is seldom visited in the park since it is a harbor seal nursing area, and as we sat in silence, the glacier gods unleashed a calving episode that i will never forget…

not just small boulder size pieces were calved but mountain-size walls of ice collapsed time and time again… it was as if an earthquake struck and this world of ice and snow was being destroyed… the amount of ice that calved i cannot imagine… the scale of that mountain of ice was beyond my comprehension, but time and time again that frozen face collapsed sending forth a swell that even our ship could feel…. even as we left, sailing slowly away through this sea of frozen ice, the glacier continued to collapse… my camera hung by my side, for i knew that i would never be able to capture the scale of what took place…

September 21, 2014

Southbound Skagway, Alaska

with the rain still falling, i took my last walk on the streets of Skagway… i enjoyed a quiet lunch with a good friend and as lunch ended, we both shared a sad good-bye till another summer… i left Skagway with so many beautiful memories… memories of a train ride taken with Joanne who now waits for me to return… we napped and watched the Yukon pass slowly by in those moments we shared… there were so many trips with friends as we walked the forest around Chilkoot Lake… i regretted though the many walks in the forest that were never taken as there were just not enough summer days… i will remember always that section of the historic Chilkoot Trail that my boots did tread hoping someday i can finish the trail up a Lake Bennet in the Yukon… and of the bears, i leave with mixed emotions… are we loving the bears and whales too much… do we need to give them both more space… by the end of the summer i choose not to watch either of you as i only want to see you both in a solitude with nature… tonight in the dark we will cast our lines and sail away from the docks of Skagway… i will miss you all in so many little ways… sailing southbound again i remember walking the deck and turning one last time bidding you farewell until another summer…

September 24, 2014
Southbound Queen Charlotte Sound
off the coast of B.C.

and the rain followed us all the way to Vancouver, but first i must reflect back a few days…

September 21, 2014
Juneau

Juneau met us with rains throughout the day, but after a do-nothing morning, i put on my rain boots with my raincoat and walked the streets of Juneau for the last time this summer… memories of my whales came flooding back, time after time… i remembered the many solitary hours we shared in each other's company… and of my walks, there were many good walks, walks in which i shared my solitude only with my boots… the crowded streets, a parade of voyagers hurrying about… i walked thru your masses in silence, for this is not the Juneau i care to remember… jewelry stores hawking their goods… the barkers standing at the doors hailing you like some prostitute advertising her goods… i would much rather have seen one of the many bars that silently vanished in the night because of these stores… these stores that now are a symbol of the exploitation brought about by the ships that i call my home all summer long… the rain felt good falling, cleansing my spirit, while the puddles were fun to splash through like a child… we left Juneau only to hit strong winds and even heavier rains but i didn't care as i was southbound to my little haven called Ketchikan…

September 23, 2014
Ketchikan

Ketchikan gave us our only day of sun on our southbound journey from Whittier: therefore, my reflection as i wandered did not have me in my rain boots… i wandered to the grocery store only to purchase my Hostess Dinettes as they are the one vice i choose not to give up this summer… with them securely packed away in my backpack, i took my last walk into the town… to Monica and my friends at Crazy Wolf Studio, i will miss you and thank you for keeping me in the company of the ravens as now my raven amulet will keep me in its embrace throughout the long days of winter… i bought only a sweatshirt and t-shirt with the name of my beloved little Ketchikan on them as they will remind me of my piece of paradise thousands of miles away… eventually i found myself at our ship's gangway, hesitating as if i could avoid my fate… i regretfully walked the gangway onto our ship… my boots cried out for the streets, to wander them without the masses of humanity, as this is my little piece of heaven, a part of heaven that i choose not to share… i stood in silence on the decks as we casted off our lines and slowly drifted from the dock… i then found myself looking from the stern as visions of my Ketchikan slowly faded away… soon i would be out of Alaskan waters for yet another year…

> But now it comes to distances and
> both of us must try
> Your eyes are soft with sorrow
> Hey that's no way to say good-bye
>
> Leonard Cohen

September 25, 2014
Southbound Vancouver, B.C.

the lines have been cast off… i'm on the final leg of my journey now… it will be a short sail out the Straits of Juan de Fuca, then around Cape Flattery keeping Tatoosh Island well to our Port, then it's a downwind sail to the Potato Patch, the rough waters, just before passing under the Golden Gate Bridge and into San Francisco…yes i'm homeward bound with only two wake-ups left…

October 3, 2014
Sun City West, Az.

i am once again home… Joanne is by my side, and it feels so good, her scent, her touch, the sound of her voice…. and of my Joshua, he has returned, my constant companion with his unconditional love… how can i forget the moment my shuttle pulled up to our house… there in the window sat Joshua, hoping then realizing his wish came true, his friend had returned…. the days quickly flew by as i returned to patterns, habits that i longed to begin again… i sit once again on our patio in the morning, reading while Joanne is at her desk within my view…. my birds are happy as they feed once again, and yes, Joshua rests by my side…

it was a good summer and in a way i miss Alaska… i miss my many friends… and always, as i think of my summer in Alaska, the image that returns time and time again is that image of my little town of Ketchikan fading from my view as i sail southbound…

Selections from
Wilderness Essays: Volume 1

A Special Hike for a
Lost Friend

October 18, 1980

Once again i stood at the canyon's rim and stared at its inner depths, it's such a beautiful place… every time i focus on its beauty, it becomes so much more… today i knew that my hike would be so much different, so much more special…i hesitated to start but i knew i must… and this time, the first of my many trips down, i glanced at Joanne… her support was there for me… my pack held not its usual load, but a very special one, one which i had grown to love and admire… today my backpack held so much love from so many people, and a very special part of us all… on this day i carried my father's ashes to his final resting … i felt honored that i was the one who took this journey, for only i touched a very special part of him with this canyon… he will always be such a part of my canyon days… i walked the trail now for the two of us… today i walked it with my father closer to me than i had ever felt… my usual pace was slower, and i looked upon this canyon differently today… i prayed the canyon's spirit appreciated this task that i had to do- i hoped it felt strongly my father's presence… i knew he was with me, helping me as i took this journey… thoughts changed from memories to prayer and always back again to this canyon… i told my father its story once again, but now i knew he understood it all so much more… each part of this trail brought back memories from a year ago when the two of us fulfilled a dream of his… that special dream he held on to for so many years… i met two who made that dream a reality, a wrangler who led our string of mules into the canyon, and Hank, the mule my father rode… i wished dearly that they had come today also to bid their own farewell… finally my destination came

75

closer- i wished it was further, but i knew what i had to do… as i stood upon the spot, i began the task i had to perform… from my pack i took my bible and my father's ashes… i sat on a cliff and read aloud the words of God… i wanted to continue to read, to put off what i had to do… finally i opened the small box and handled it so very carefully, for they were so sacred to me, the ashes of my father… i prayed to God and to my father as i slowly threw each handful of ash into the wind… they showered the rocks and fell within the canyon's most inner depth… they fell upon my feet and upon the alter i had made…

my father was now at rest- a part of one of God's most treasured creations… from this spot i saw phantom ranch, the river and the canyon that surrounded us… i didn't want to leave now, as earlier i didn't want to arrive, but i knew my life had to continue… later from a higher viewpoint, i watched hikers as they walked to the spot that i had released my father's ashes from… i hoped they were praising the canyon before them… then as quickly as they arrived, they left… i was thankful that my father would always be able to praise this canyon and now would never have to leave… my walk home was lonely and hard… i felt empty as i left a very special person behind, yet i knew that i could always return… i will always love my father and he will always live within me…

i'll always walk this canyon- and someday i hope my final journey will find us both reunited- and then i'll help Fred, my son, with his lonely walk home… i love you dad… i believe in you and all you stood for, and i pray in thanks that i was blessed to carry your name and be your son…

"Jesus said unto her, I am the resurrection, and the life: he that believeth in me, though he were dead, yet shall he live: And whosoever liveth and believeth in me shall never die. Believeth thou this?"

King James Version: John 11: 25-26

Excerpts from: Summer Winds: an Odyssey of Dreams and a Road Well-Traveled

Highway 1 Northbound: Our first Real Summer Vacation"

Preface to a long drive north for years since i began teaching in 1982, i needed to supplement our income… so besides teaching, i coached two sports at Horizon High School, JV football and freshmen wrestling, then during the school year at nights, when i could, i worked odd shifts at our local Circle K store… when the school year ended, i worked full time till the school year began again, so my summer vacations really meant just long days working at Circle K… i continued to work on improving my salary by enrolling in a Master's program at Nova University… as my salary slowly increased i began to work less and less at Circle K and imagined summers filled with vacations…

for years i always dreamed of taking a long road trip with Joanne, camping and hoteling our way up the west coast… we often talked about that trip at our dinner table, but never thought it would actually happen… i wanted to see the ocean again, redwood trees, mountains, and the coast of California, Oregon and Washington… also deep down, ever since i was a kid, i wanted to go to Alaska…

Doug MacCarter was a colleague of mine at Horizon High School and was an exceptional wildlife biologist in addition to being a biology teacher… Doug had worked as a park ranger up in Montana, was involved in numerous biological field studies, one being with the grizzly bears in Yellowstone with the Graighead brothers (Frank and John Graighead, over a thirteen year period did the first major study of grizzly bears in the United States). Doug's graduate work included a major study of the osprey on Flathead Lake in Montana… Doug and his brother Butch were influenced by Rachel Carson's book, *Silent Spring,* and sought out to see if insecticides were a factor for why the osprey population around Flathead Lake was crashing… a bond formed between Doug and me during my first few years at Horizon and eventually we both talked about going to Alaska… we started talking more seriously and decided to drive up to Alaska during the summer of 1989… at first i planned to meet Doug at his cabin on Flathead Lake, Montana, but started thinking that instead of just driving straight to Montana, this would be an ideal time for Joanne and i to take our Highway 1 road trip…

throughout the 1988-1989 school year, Doug and i planned our drive to Alaska also including a lot of hiking with the highlight of our trip being a canoe trip across Admiralty Island, Alaska, better known as the Fortress of the Bears, and the bears being Alaskan brown bears… countless trips were taken to REI to update and purchase more of my hiking and backpacking gear plus outfit Joanne for our drive up the coast…

June 14, 1989
Ventura, California

there were many hours spent dreaming, planning and looking through tour books to plan our adventure north along highway 1… this included the many nights i would go over our trip in my mind when i should have been sleeping, but now the day of our departure actually came…

yesterday went by so quickly… i took my Jeep CJ7 in for its final checkup before heading, not only to Washington, but also to Alaska… Dave, our auto mechanic, gave me a box-load of parts that would typically fail during a long hard road trip… then there was the final list of jobs on my honey-do-list that needed to be addressed… one last check on the trailer i would pull as i tried to ensure everything was not only in the trailer, but also packed correctly…

Looking at all the gear and supplies that we loaded, i couldn't believe that there were still all the last minute items that needed to be loaded… the last task of the day was when i took our little pets, Jennie and Denali, to the kennel… it was always hard looking at their little eyes as they pleaded with us not to go… i went to bed early last night mainly because i was so nervous about our trip working out…

as we now listened to the hum of the tires, Joanne and i realized we were finally on our trip, but along with the road noise we both had that nervous feeling, will everything go alright, will the trailer work out, will the Jeep run as expected… in the early hours of our drive, i constantly checked the Jeep's gauges and looked in the rearview mirror to see that everything was alright with the trailer… as i began to slowly relax we listened to music, from a tape i had made, and finally the music filled our souls and lifted our spirits… the miles rolled by with the music playing and soon we crossed the Arizona state line into Blythe, California, and all was going well… our vacation was finally here… Blythe lead us to Indio and on to Palm Springs… to our amazement the mountains were covered with an army of wind turbines… as this was our first road trip into California, all this scenery was new and exciting… we passed San Bernardino on Interstate 10 and then the traffic started to build up, highway traffic that neither Joanne and i were use to driving in… now my excitement was overcome with the stress of traffic, the pollution and searching the highway's signs to ensure we were still on the correct interstate highway…   the afternoon now slowly passed but excitement was stirring in my heart as i saw a sign that stated we were on the Ventura Highway… i fumbled through my music collection and listened to America's album, Highway and the song Ventura Highway… music filled my soul as we now began our search for our highway exit… before long Joanne finally saw our exit for Highway 101, i knew the coast was not too far ahead… Welcome to Ventura… Joanne and i smiled at each other as we knew we made it through Day 1… salt air filled my lungs as a symphony of cries from the gulls welcomed us to the ocean once again… Joanne and i both grew up close to the ocean in New Jersey and we have missed it dearly since moving to Arizona in 1976… we took a little trip to the harbor so i could see all the boats, as boats filled my youth… all the sailboats reminded me of my first sailboat after i sold Little Tal, my very first boat… i was only 12 years old and now owned my first of many sailboats… we wandered down to the pier and took our first photo of each other then took a walk on the beach… after our first meal of fresh fish we headed back to our motel room to plan for our next day's adventure and to make my first journal entry…

i was thinking of all we will would see on this journey… the mountains and the sea, what could be better… i am so lucky, i can only hope i take this journey slowly and look with my father's eyes at everything we shall see… remember the little things i hope to always recall and enjoy years later as i'm enjoying it now… take it slowly… remember to look at all the rocks but don't forget to smell the roses of this journey…

June 15, 1989
Big Sur, California

today i truly saw how beautiful the mountains and sea can be when they are painted in one masterpiece… from the beaches of Ventura, eventually to the forest of Big Sur, my eyes witnessed both worlds…

we started our day early knowing we would eat breakfast later in the town of Santa Barbara… once our tires were humming on the road, and i finished my constant watch of the Jeep's gauges and the trailer, and found that everything was alright i was able to relax a little more… i slid a tape, Crosby, Stills and Nash, in our recorder and listened to my tunes as we began to put the first of the day's miles behind us… with my window open i was able to smell the ocean air and it brought back so many memories of trips to the beach in New Jersey as a youth… as we left Manahawkin, New Jersey, we rode over the causeway bridge that spanned the salt marshes and back bays... all the car's windows would be immediately rolled down so we could smell the salt air as we were within miles of the ocean...

Joanne spotted The Big Yellow House, a restaurant that was recommended to us from one of our many travel books we brought along for this trip... i had purchased a red Sierra West canvas bag that we kept all of our travel books in... besides all my Roadside Geology Guides, we included our AAA books and several Sunset Magazine books, one each for California, Oregon and Washington... right on the wooden console i had built, next to my seat, i had a holder for my mug of hot tea and our AAA road guide that would be our road bible throughout this summer...

we left highway 1 to join the 101 so we could see the little town of Solvang with its windmills... there were so many little places that we both wanted to stop at, like Pea Soup Anderson's, where Joanne's parents told us we must take the time to enjoy a cup of their soup, but unfortunately we had too many miles to cover... we eventually joined the coast highway again around Pismo Beach... Joanne kept yelling at me to keep my eyes on the road, but i was like a little kid in a toy store, constantly looking at the scenery on either side of the highway... we did stop at the little fishing town of Morro Bay with its ancient volcanic mound that stood as a sentry at the mouth of its harbor... nestled on the coast, Morro Bay was a beautiful little haven, one that i knew i could spend a lifetime living in... looking at the beach in Morro Bay made me want so badly to walk the beach and get closer to the rocks, especially that rock that guarded the harbor of Morro Bay... rocks became an important part of my world ever since i completed my degree in geology, and i planned to add to my rock collection throughout our summer odyssey up the coast...

later in the day, as we entered the incredible world of Big Sur, with its redwood trees, and truly where the mountains meet the sea, we took a walk along Pfeiffer Beach... i could not have imagined how beautiful this part of California would be... earlier in the day i finally saw and touched my first redwood tree... these were trees that have stood for hundreds of years... my hands, like the hands of a child constantly touched not only the bark but all the needles and cones that had fallen from this creation... i constantly arched my neck back to see the tops of these gentle giants... i could not believe that trees could be so tall and beautiful...

i sit now on the little porch of a cabin we rented for the night, and write my thoughts of the day that passed... i love the desert but always in my heart i wished i lived either in the mountains or along the coast... the sea has the ability to bring a special joy to my heart... its magic has always worked wonders on me ever since i was that kid spending my summers in Beach Haven West, New Jersey... it may be the cries of the gulls, the salt air, or the ocean water, and whether it be the gray waters of the Atlantic, the blue-green waters along the coast of the Gulf of Mexico, or now the vibrant colors of the Pacific, these were the colors that painted this beautiful masterpiece i now admired... i do truly love the desert, and leaving it would mean i must lose my beautiful canyon, the canyon where i put my father's ashes and the canyon trails my boots have come to love... but today, right in these moments my heart screams for this ocean.. maybe the lesson to learn here, is each of these worlds has its own special meaning to me, don't try to compare the beauty of these creations but simply enjoy, for the moment, each one to its fullest... there is so much beauty that my eyes have taken for granted and because of that caused me to not appreciate what i saw in that moment... there are far too many times i stopped and pretended to view its beauty, but all too often schedules and time quickened my pace... there have been many vistas when i wanted to stop and become a part of, but the onward pull of time, a villain that for me is so hard to conquer, always wins out... i must learn patience

June 16, 1989
Monterey, California

so many faces of the ocean we saw today but one that will always be remembered was my first drive over Bixby Bridge, along the coast of Big Sur… the bridge was completed in 1932 and is reported to be "one of the highest bridges of its kind in the world, soaring 260 feet above the bottom of a steep canyon carved by Bixby Creek…" and i will confess, much to Joanne's dislike, as she is afraid of narrow winding roads along any type of road that has an exposure of more than a few feet, i crossed the bridge then did a U-turn so i could do it once again… it was hard to keep my eyes on the road as i wanted to take in all of the scenery… i'm sure i crossed the divided highway more than once, but really it couldn't be helped, and besides the scenery was so beautiful… words couldn't be found to describe my feelings as i drove across this bridge… so many prayers of thanks have been said during our trip, as i truly was seeing creation at its finest… yes the Grand Canyon is breathtaking but how do i compare these masterpieces, it's just not possible, and each of these creations needed their own prayers of thanks… John Muir spoke often of nature, in a religious sense, and believed nature to be God's greatest gift… i guess my prayers reflected my beliefs regarding nature and these beliefs that i hold are very similar to Muir's…

leaving Big Sur we soon entered the area of Monterey and our guide books told us Monterrey's 17 Mile Drive was a must… i will not even try to describe my feelings of joy and excitement… we stopped at Pebble Beach Golf Course, thinking of Joanne's father but also i had to see how this golf course weaved its way along this portion of the coast… i would have loved to play a round of golf there today and would have willingly paid the 200 dollars but once again there was just not enough time… leaving the 17 Mile Drive, we soon found our motel in the Cannery Row section of Monterey… i picked a beautiful Victorian style hotel as i wanted this to be a big treat for Joanne…

June 18, 1989

Crescent City, California

the sea has now shown all its glory from the steep cliffs of Big Sur, all the way up the coast to Pt. Arena… i had a hard time comprehending how beautiful and diverse a coastline could be, for most of my life i drove the east coast from New Jersey to Florida which is composed mostly of flat barrier islands… there are no mountains to be seen along the coast… the only mountains along the east coast are the ancient and well weathered summits of the Appalachian Mountains, and they are 50 miles inland from the coast… but along this western coastline i saw not a confrontation between the sea and the mountains, but that the results when they join hands is a peaceful harmony, each one bringing out and displaying the beauty of the other to its fullest… the sea would not have been as dramatic without the mountains, and the same could be said for the mountains in regards to the sea… the sea has carved its signature unto the mountains and the mountains stood bold because of the sea…

there were some beautiful little towns, the brightest would have to be Mendocino with its Victorian touch… a town for the artist and it's no wonder, living there would inspire anyone… i stood by its little harbor, nestled in the rocks and listened to the wind and the ocean in a symphony with the gulls… in the distance was the clanging of a harbor buoy…

then just as the mountains and sea are becoming your soulmates, in walks the forest… and it was not just any forest, but a forest composed of the tallest trees found anywhere on earth, the redwoods… we drove through a protected area of this forest called the Avenue of the Giants, a 31 mile drive that was like driving through a cathedral created by God … it was a sin that a highway had to make an ugly scar within this forest… at one point i pulled over to the side and told Joanne i had to walk within this forest… the forest floor was carpeted with the needles of these and other trees... i walked slowly and silently so my boots would not leave their mark... i made a promise to myself that i had to walk within the forests now of both Yosemite and Sequoia National Parks...

tonight we set up in a little camping cabin in a KOA campground with redwoods all around... my table was a redwood stump... i tried to count the rings of growth but got sadden by the thought of the greed of man destroying this and so many other forests... tomorrow i will leave the state of California and with that my newfound friend, the redwoods... the northern most limit of the redwoods are right along the California-Oregon border...

as i say good-by to California there are so many pictures i etched in my memory... the Golden Gate Bridge... it's all they say it is and so much more with the fog that was sweeping in from the sea, and within its bay stood quietly a fortress of rock called Alcatraz... i crossed the fault of all faults, the San Andreas Fault, and stood where it entered the sea... today the fault was quiet but its power and fury will always be felt... and California, i will always remember your harbors with their boats that take gently the bounty from the sea and the mountains that framed your coastline... a coastline that only time could create... and to the gentle giants, my beautiful redwood trees, i will sleep the last time amongst you tonight, and a peaceful sleep it will be...

so to you California, i bid a farewell, but i promise i will walk gently along your coast again... tomorrow the anticipation of a new friend, Oregon...

June 20, 1989

Astoria KOA, Oregon

such diversity has abounded us during this trip, from the cacti of the Sonoran Desert, to the rocky coastline of California, with its cold, blue-green ocean joining hand-in-hand with fog-shrouded forests of redwood trees...

yesterday we began to see the many faces of another new friend, the coast of Oregon... thinking back over the last few days, i realize it was hard saying goodbye to California… all i knew of our next state in this journey came from the beautiful featured photos in our Sunset travel magazine on Oregon… the photos showed beautiful beaches with fortresses, or should i say mountains of rock just off the coast… my geology studies told me these were all remnants of ancient volcanoes… are there more rocks now to add to my collection, time and the miles will tell… still i think, how could anything ever be created more perfect than California where the forest and sea were in harmony…

the coast of Oregon came into view, in the early morning hours, while traveling along a highway and looking out on an ocean partially hidden by a silent fog bank… i needed Oregon to be different from California for it to be remembered as the next segment of our coastline odyssey, and it was… the sky overcast at times… clouds and an intermittent thick fog dancing a ballet… there were times when the clouds were dominant, but then they faded as a fog crept in from the sea blanketing endless beaches bordered by sand dunes… the air was damp with a coldness that seeped right through you… sweatshirts and sweaters replaced our t-shirts from the past days… would this be our new reflection traveling up this coast…

the coast of Oregon began with its beautiful beaches and what always seemed like a gentle surf… driving north we could see the coast taking on an entirely different landscape… one enters a world where the mountains, forest and sea all join hands… at times the coastline is composed of cliffs covered with the firs, spruce and hemlock trees of this temperate rainforest… the highway winding its way through mountains and forests… standing out along the prominent viewpoints are always the lighthouses… coastal angels that protect those that harvest the bounty of the sea… i sit and view these lighthouses strictly as ornaments decorating this coast, yet how many worried eyes prayed to see their beacon of safety shining through the fog warning them of an angry coast… the lighthouses of Oregon will always be remembered (probably because Joanne's new sweatshirt had etchings depicting all of Oregon's lighthouses)… as a child i always loved our vacation trip to see Barnegat Lighthouse, on the northern end of Long Beach Island in New Jersey… did these lighthouses remind me of my summers on a different coast, one not of mountains and forests but one composed of barrier beaches…

last night we spent the night in a beautiful beachfront motel in Florence… after i feasted on a dinner of Dungeness crabs, we sat on our little patio and listened to the surf and watched yet another beautiful sunset… tonight we are camping in a KOA campground, far enough from the ocean so i will not have the sound of the surf to put me to sleep

June 21, 1989
Crescent Lake, just outside the boundary of Olympic National Park, Washington

our day began early with an scenic drive across the Astoria-Megler Bridge connecting Astoria, Oregon, with Megler, Washington… our AAA guide book told us the bridge opened 23 years ago in 1966, and is said to be the longest continuous truss bridge in North America (a truss bridge is a bridge whose load-bearing super-structure is composed of a truss, or a structure of connected elements, usually forming triangular units)… the bridge was a little over 4 miles long and reported to be the last completed segment of Highway 101 between Los Angles, California, and Olympia, Washington… driving across this bridge took me back to my college days and the many drives i took over the 20 mile long Chesapeake Bay Bridge… as we drove across the bridge there was a seagull flying over the water, level with our eyesight, and only a short distance from the bridge… the bird, keeping pace with my Jeep, hardly flapped its wings, seeming to glide on wind currents… i had difficulty keeping my eyes on the road, i would have much rather watched my feathered friend in its amazing display of flight…

the state of Washington is nicknamed the Evergreen State and it was easy to see why… throughout the day the forests seemed greener and more immense than i have yet seen, for everywhere i looked it was this brilliant dark green color from the evergreens that blanketed the hills and roadside, yet i knew, just to the east of the Olympic Peninsula i would once again find my mountains and hopefully see the white icy summit of Mt. Rainier…we began our drive, in the this new state, wandering out on the Long Beach Peninsula, in lower western Washington… here once again, i saw the Pacific Ocean and the miles of beaches that my bare feet wanted to walk… i knew, from looking at our road atlas, that for the rest of our travels the coastline, and its ocean, would be lost from our view… deep in my heart i knew this scenery needed to be enjoyed now before i lost it for the rest of our journey…

as we drove north from Aberdeen, to our destination just on the outskirts of Olympic National Park, i was troubled by the countless number of logging trucks that traveled down this highway… i kept thinking, "will there be any trees left before the greed of the logging industry takes all of them… yet i knew in my heart, besides me, there were countless others that also had the need or thirst for the lumber and paper produced from these trees…a lesson learned, be careful where i pointed my finger of blame…

later in the day we checked into our room in the Crescent Lake lodge… while Joanne relaxed in a wooden chair out on the lawn looking out on Crescent Lake, i took to the rainforest… its canopy of trees, so thick and green, with a multitude of ferns and moss carpeting the forest floor, not only welcomed me but called for my boots to touch its soul… a short hike to a waterfall allowed me to see a small part of this world… my hands, like a child, wanted to run across the bark of these new trees, touching and smelling their essence… i wanted so much to begin to identify all these ferns as i felt a need to know their names, yet i held back from this task maybe out of reverence, for this forest and its spirit touched my soul in a new way… the solitude this forest bestowed on me felt so different…

my walk was short, yet i stopped and ate to lengthen my stay… eventually i found my way homeward and as i looked over my shoulder i said a farewell, for it may be many rains and snows before i walk this path again…

Washington has found a place in my heart…

June 24, 1989

Seattle, Washington: our final destination the lodge at Crescent Lake… so many memories of that little lodge will be held dear… our room, at the top of the stairs and just to the left… the window that we looked out onto that beautiful lake… the wooden Adirondack chairs that we sat in, napping and dreaming of days to come… was it the simplicity of the lodge that stole our hearts or the green forest that it slept within… whatever it was, we fell deeply in love with that lodge… at times it brought back ancient memories, Medford Lake Lodge, in Medford, New Jersey … it was the night of our wedding, a snow storm was blowing outside and we sat by the lodge's fireplace, keeping warm and dreaming of our life to be…

it was hard leaving the lodge in the morning, but we were also anxious to finally see the city of Seattle, and my sister Jennifer… she lived in Seattle while attending the University of Washington, and talked constantly of how we had to visit this city… we left the lodge and entered Olympic National Park just outside of the city of Port Angeles, as i wanted to drive up to Hurricane Ridge to view the icy peaks of the Olympic Mountains… the road to our destination was covered in low clouds with a mist of rain silently falling on our windshield… as we slowly found our way up the mountain, the clouds just kept getting thicker and thicker until finally at the end of the road all we could see were our hands in front of our faces… the beauty of Mt. Olympia with its glacier covered peaks will have to wait for another day and another dream…

we followed Highway 101 to its end in the city of Olympia, then once again found the traffic and congestion associated with major highways… we followed Interstate 405 north until we could see the skyline of the city of Seattle… we now searched frantically for the exit my sister told us to take, so we could finally meet up in a Bed and Breakfast that we all rented for the next few days… our excitement grew as we left the highway and entered the city… there before our eyes was the famous Space Needle built in 1962, and i could understand why, next to the Eiffel Tower in France, it is considered one of the most photographed structures… now we began to see the many faces this city had to offer… our Bed and Breakfast was located right near Green Lake which my sister said she often walked through… Joanne and i at once agreed that we could learn to love this city and to live here someday, but then how many times have we said that in the last few weeks…

my sister took us to Pete's Fish and Chips for our dinner so that we could afterwards walk along the water's edge… this little fish stand was a special place in her years living in Seattle as she could always walk the beach adjacent to this little fish stand… i would soon learn that Seattle is surrounded by water… always as we traveled around this new city, i kept looking far towards the east… i knew there in the clouds slept my mountains, Mt. Rainier and Mt. Baker… on a day when the sky is blue and clouds are few these mountains, like sentinels of rock and glaciers, come out and look protectively over this beautiful city… it was hard to believe that mountains i had often dreamed of seeing were now hidden right before my eyes…

often in our quiet moments , during these past few days, Joanne and i would relive our journey as we recalled all the places that were special to each of us… we have been so fortunate and blessed during our odyssey up the coast and i think of all that will soon come to be as i head to Alaska… my gypsy soul has traveled many miles over the years and especially with these summer winds … i have always counted my blessings with Joanne as she has always allowed me the freedom to see every aspect of this world i live within… to her i will always be indebted, and my only way to repay her is with the love i can give to her in return, but i can never match the loved she has given to me…

i am sadden that this part of my journey has ended… tomorrow morning i will take Joanne to the airport for her lonely flight back to our waiting pets… and for me, well it's off to Alaska…

Excerpts from an Alaskan Journey: Denali National Park

July 7, 1989
Fairbanks Alaska

today a part of this journey came to its end… this road that led us on our adventure northward, within the course of several miles, lost its charm and excitement as we were consumed with everyday traffic… where was our parade of vagabonds who met each night and talked of our adventures throughout the days that passed… as old friends left this highway, for other distant points, there were always new friends joining us on this journey… this road, the Alaskan Highway, began in the Canadian town of Dawson Creek, 1,309 miles away… looking out amongst this traffic my thoughts were of a more noble and fitting end rather than this chaotic mix of cars driven by the multitude of unfamiliar faces… my mood was uplifted slightly as we stopped by the monument that was testimony to this highway's ending, but without the excitement of days gone by, the typical tourist photos were taken… the other famous statue, in downtown Fairbanks, titled "the unknown First Family" was eventually found… the sculpture showed two native Alaskans, a child standing next to an adult with their husky dog… all the images stared out at you with a defiant look showing their pride of being native in this land of snow… more photos were taken… as a part of a journey ends, you realize once again, that the journey will always live longer in your memory than the destination… looking downward from that sculpture, with a tear in my eyes, prayers of thanks for a safe journey were whispered…

as one road ended, another one began, and with that a new journey… Doug's and my quest now was to see the icy, storm swept summit of Denali (Denali, a native term meaning the Great One, was not the original name given by the white man to this mountain, the tallest peak in North America. The first non-native name, given by a Yukon gold prospector was Densmore Mountain, but it is unknown why that individual's name was chosen. The name McKinley was first used after William Dickey, another Yukon prospector who wrote the name in an 1897 New York Sun article. Dickey was an admirer of President McKinley)

July 8, 1989
Denali National Park

our journey now headed south, on the George Parks Highway, towards Denali (George Parks was an American engineer who worked in the Alaskan Territory and became its first resident governor)… this drive was only two and a half hours south of Fairbanks and adjacent, for the most part, to the famous Alaska Railroad… while driving south i looked frantically at times to see one of the trains carrying passengers from Fairbanks to Denali National Park… this experience, along with the Trans Canadian Railroad, were on Joanne's and my bucket list of train rides we wanted to experience… as Doug and i came closer to the park, the cloudy horizon was desperately searched for Denali, but as fate would have it, the mountain would not be seen… regardless a new beauty was surrounding us… the forest that blanketed the landscape was one not witnessed before, as it was marked by trees, dwarfed in their size due to the long, hard northern winters they faced… this was my first experience of seeing a Taiga Forest (the Taiga forest circles the northern latitudes of the earth, and are represented by trees, dwarfed in size and in a forest of low density)… regardless, this forest was of a vastness never before witnessed, and in its background, partly hidden by the clouds, stood the Alaskan Range, guardian of the northern frontier…

with great excitement the sign was finally seen informing one that you were now entering Denali National Park (the park, established in 1917, was originally named Mt. McKinley National

Park, but was renamed Denali National Park and Preserve when the park was enlarged to include complete ecosystems in 1980)... without even thinking, the jeep was pulled over to the side of the road, and like the typical tourists, one by one, our photos were taken by the sign ... once again the horizon was scanned, but still no view of Denali... from all my years of hiking in the outdoors, experience has taught the lesson that one must learn the ways of nature and have patience with it... if the mountain chooses for one to bear witness to its beauty, treasure that gift with reverence, and a prayer of thanks should always be whispered... but still, i waited with the eagerness and excitement of a child on Christmas morning to finally see Denali ... my dream is to one day have my boots walk on that summit, but all my readings have shown that very few people, even with all the technical skills necessary to achieve that goal, actually can see it through, as the mountain has the final word...

tonight Doug and i sat by our tents planning and talking about the days to come... the sky ways painted with a scattering of low clouds, an arctic day was ending, but the sun still sat low in the western sky, and the mountain has yet to show its face... as my eyes soaked in this wilderness, my thoughts were of a canyon far away in the desert of Arizona... so different are their faces, yet each has its own beauty... and i wonder, how sleeps my canyon tonight, and with this, i bid goodnight to you Joanne... thank you for your love and for this freedom you have always granted to me and my boots

July 9, 1989

a campsite in Denali National Park around 4 a.m.

after awakening early and not knowing why, i lay still in a warm sleeping bag slowly gathering thoughts for the coming day... the fly to my tent was unzipped before going to sleep last night allowing the cool night air to be felt... there was only the sounds of some nearby birds... it seemed mosquitos covered every part of the tent ... did they ever go away... looking through the screen door, the predawn sky was colored a faded blue with only a scattering of clouds in sight … unzipping the screen slightly and poking my head out enabled a greater area of the sky to be scanned… frantically i searched more and more of the sky checking for clouds, but few were to be found… a thought occurred to me for this early awakening with clear skies… might it be that the mountain was calling… quickly sweat pants and a jacket were put on, but mainly to fend off the constant onslaught of mosquitoes, and i soon headed down the road… our guide book stated that one of the best places to view the summit of Denali was just a few miles from our campsite… a female moose and her calf stood by the side off the road grazing… there was not even a hint of a thought of completely stopping, as my intent was not on photographing wildlife, but on seeing an icy summit far in the distance… slowly and cautiously the moose and its calf were left behind… since the windows were unzipped, the early morning air felt cool and refreshing on my bearded face (my CJ7 Jeep had a canvas rag top, and to open the windows one had to unzip them)… now far in the distance a band of low clouds had started to form erasing anything that would be seen on the horizon… again my quest was hidden within a covering of clouds… i wanted so badly to first have witnessed its reflection alone and with a prayer, but again one must wait until the chosen time, but now the location was known as to where this snow covered mountain could be found… driving back to our campsite, thoughts ran through my mind of all that would hopefully be experienced today… it would be a beautiful day…

later in the evening today was wrapped with frustration because of what this part of our trip was becoming… we took the free bus that drove the Park Road out to Wonder Lake to once again try to see the mountain, but now with its reflection painted on the lake… the ride through this park was a nightmare, as my spirit was screaming to be set free from the moving cage, better known as a school bus… this was not the way

Doug and i had imagined or wanted to experience this wilderness… the people who surrounded us did not have the eyes or spirit of John Muir, one who found reverence with nature… no, now every object of nature was loudly being counted… they did not witness the essence of a moose but instead, it just became a statistic that they all recorded… the noise was ripping my heart apart… all of a sudden, for an instant, and without rhyme or reason, the mountain shone on the distant horizon… depressed that our first glimpse of the mountain had to be witnessed like this with people climbing over seats and each other only to catch a quick glimpse and photo… did they even realized what they had just witnessed, or was this too another statistic to be added to their list…

after an hour or so, that lasted for what seemed like an eternity, Doug and i grabbed our daypacks and left the bus to venture into the wilderness to find some peace (all along the Park Road were points where day hikers or backpackers could leave the outbound bus to Wonder Lake only to catch the inbound bus at a later time)… this was the way that we both had intended to witness this park.. our boots now fought their way through waist-high alder that covered the many hillsides… mosquitoes, sweat and the threat of coming into contact with an Alaskan grizzly bear became our world… as funny as it seemed, peace was now being felt… a small summit was eventually reached which enabled us to get an idea of the vastness of this wilderness… by scanning the horizon, it became obvious that the back country of Denali National Park was too large to fully grasp and i was too ignorant of its ways to really hike any part of this park (there are no established hiking trails in the park, a policy that was established to keep the fragile tundra plant life intact and to keep it from being destroyed by a constant trampling of boots that would quickly harm the vegetation with no hope of ever recovering and returning. In this National Park, unlike any other park, everything had to be experienced hiking cross country with an excellent knowledge of outdoor skills including the use of a map and compass.)… after several hours of hiking we found our way back to the Park Road and walked along the roadside waiting for our next bus ride.

Once again the bus ride was an uncensored assortment of loud noises that one wished not to hear… i thought again about this wilderness, stretching endlessly in all directions, was it calling out to me, or just haunting and teasing my boots… the bus drove onward, and because of all the unwanted chatter, the minutes slowly turned into hours with the noise never ceasing… eventually the bus pulled into a turnout overlooking a mountain range far in the distant… the Polychrome Mountains consist of many multicolored strata of rocks… the Polychrome Mountains resulted from volcanism that occurred millions of years in the past, and each of the colored strata recorded separate events of volcanic activity… looking at this mountain reminded me of the many volcanic outcrops studied as a geology student at Arizona State University… with a rock hammer and hand lens we dissected so many of these outcrops to better understand their history… time and time again, i wanted to walk these hills rather than return to the confinement of the noisy bus… did these passengers even see what my eyes saw, or better yet, did they even care what was painted before them, since there was nothing out there to add to their list of "things they saw"…

this day ended with so many mixed emotions, but knowing, that if there was to be any intention of seeing this vastness of nature surrounding us, the bus was our only answer…

July 10, 1989
Savage River campground, Denali Park

today Doug and i ventured to a new campground a little further within the park, as we were both trying to escape the swarms of tourists that have invaded the park, yet are we not also a part of what we are running from… there were mixed feelings after yesterday's experiences, should we just leave this wilderness and head towards our next destination, or stay… no, we had to stay, because as John Muir said "the mountains were calling and i must go…" so now at least one more attempt had to be made to see this wilderness...

this new campground was more peaceful as spruce trees and brush made up the area the camping sites were located in... a moderately easy hike along an old gravel road led down to the Savage River... this campground and the one at Wonder Lake were the only two in the park where it was possible to view Denali if the skies were clear... now even as nice as this new location was, we still found it impossible to escape the thick clouds of mosquitos... compromises one must make to find a peace of heart...

since Doug and i were unable to take a private vehicle on the Park Road to drive out to Wonder Lake, we were forced, once again, to seek out the school buses... a different chemistry of people made this ride seem quieter, more respectful of the solitude and reverence that nature should be afforded... we did spot the usual wildlife: moose, caribou, dall sheep, and even two grizzly bears... it was scary looking at the size of these Alaskan grizzlies compared to the smaller grizzlies in Yellowstone, and to think we were just in this same area yesterday hiking... these bears were now feeding on a caribou by the creek we also had crossed yesterday... this made one think, just maybe we had the mountain gods on our side after all...

the ride out to Wonder Lake was never ending and at one point our bus stopped to let some park rangers pass us on the road (the Park Road is only a one lane highway as the road proceeded further into the park, and vehicles were always pulling over to let other vehicles pass)... Doug heard the rangers informing the bus driver that they were going out to check on a beaver den that had been observed in an area close by... Doug struck up a conversation with the rangers, and before i knew it, Doug and the rangers were off to check on the beaver's den, and informing me we would meet up again at Wonder Lake...

meanwhile the bus drive went on and on... i enjoyed scanning the vastness of the tundra landscape, as it brought back fond memories of the many hikes taken in the tundra while being stationed in Greenland with the Air Force... at times short naps were taken, only to realize nothing really changed in the scenery...

well as fate would have it, we never saw Wonder Lake, but instead i had the unfortunate luck to experience the famous "bus crash of 89" in Denali National Park...

a long drive in the confines of a school bas where the windows can't really be opened fully will tend to make the bus stuffy and the passengers sleepy... one by one our bus load of passengers were dozing off and that included me, but it should not include the bus driver... since my seat was right behind the driver, any oncoming traffic could easily be spotted... waking up after a short nap i noticed another bus approaching us (when two buses approach from opposite directions on this one lane gravel road the outbound bus, which in this case was our bus, is to pull off the road and stop to allow for the other bus to pass safely)... i watched in disbelief as our bus did not pull over but kept heading right towards the other bus... thoughts occurred, was our driver actually playing chicken with the other bus driver... time seemed to slow down and almost stopped right before the buses collided... instinctively my hands grabbed a bar bracing for the impending crash, and crash we did, right into the front of the other bus... the people in our bus, enjoying their nap were automatically thrown around the bus due to the collision, followed by screams of pain and questions on what had happened... having limited first aid training i immediately tried to assess who was seriously hurt while telling people not to move if they were hurt... our now awaken bus driver started yelling at the other bus driver as if it was his fault when it was our bus driver who fell asleep... the other bus driver immediately notified any rangers in the area to immediately come and assist in helping the injured... it was getting pretty crazy in our bus trying to help people while keeping everybody stationary... then before i knew it, our bus door flew open and a passenger from the other bus, who just happened to be a doctor, came to our rescue... within 10 minutes a ranger truck pulled up and there was Doug, who the rangers had deputized to assist in this accident due to his experience from being a ranger... when all was said and done, several people, due to their injuries, were helicoptered out to a hospital in Fairbanks, and two buses were sent out to return all of us to our awaiting vehicles...

so there it was, Doug who was now removed of his services with the rangers, and myself, an unfortunate passenger in the bus accident, never saw Wonder Lake... after a can of soup for my dinner, i sat in my tent trying not to think of all that had transpired today and believing that it was impossible for anything else to go wrong on our journey...

the sound of the river in the distance brought peaceful feelings and sleep...

July 11
Savage River Campground,
Denali National Park, Alaska

the rain falls quietly now... refuge from the relentless bites of mosquitos... a cleansing of the air... the drops of rain bead up on my tent fly before forming small rivulets that cascade gently onto the rain soaked ground... i'm protected, yet i feel so fragile as i hear the rain continually fall around me... i wrap myself in my sleeping bag, delay getting up until this shower ceases.

today Doug and i planned one more attempt on accessing this wilderness by using the school buses, convinced that nothing else could possibly go wrong... arriving only minutes before its scheduled departure, the bus still had a scattering of empty seats, making it apparent this wouldn't be a full load of passengers today... making our way down the aisle, separate seats were taken as our daypacks were tossed beside us... then came the impossible task of trying to get comfortable in a school bus seat...

the early chatter, while leaving the parking lot, was about a horrible accident in the park yesterday... looking towards Doug, i saw him already chuckling while listening to all the comments about this incident that happened the day before... the longer we listened, the more the story continued to build until it finally sounded nothing like what had actually happened... at anytime during this incredible fabrication of the truth, either of us could have jumped in and clarified what had really happened, but it was too much fun listening to this version of our accident... maybe we missed the bigger accident...

today would sadly be the last full day in a wilderness that was quickly stealing my heart... staring out the window and alone in thought, i could not stop thinking about the inconceivable vastness of this preserve that was before me... so many different faces were portrayed, and with each face, it would take a lifetime of hiking to really fully understand and know... thinking back to the first moments in the park's visitor's center, and viewing the main exhibit... i stood in front of a large topographic representation of the park that portrayed its implausible immenseness... it was overwhelming... finding a hike that would give me a real feel for this wilderness, would probably be best attempted by seeking out the advice of a ranger... sadly that ranger confirmed my first impression, stating it would be an impossible task to find that one special hike, even if one had all the various technical skills necessary... thinking back to many of my previous backpacking trips, only proved the skills necessary to hike in a park which had no established trail system... with absolutely no alpine climbing or trekking experience, and never having had to forge wild, restless rivers that flowed from the meltwater of glaciers or from winter snows confirmed my realization that more skills would be required, especially navigating a route while using only map and a compass... so riding Denali's public transportation system became the easiest way to get a taste of at least part of this wilderness, and the Park

Road, with its buses, gave one an easy access to the many facets of the preserve...

after we crossed a bridge over the Tekianka River, Doug and i disembarked from the bus to do some day hiking in the hills of Cathedral Mountain... my restless spirit wanted to race up the slopes to get a better view of ragged peaks and glaciers that most surely dominated the interior of the Preserve, but the slopes were covered with alder bushes that made the process slow... Doug knew this was good grizzly habitat so insisted we proceed with caution, making sure the bears had advance notice of our presence... approaching a small summit and then looking down the lower slopes, Doug spotted a grizzly sow (a female bear) with three small cubs... since the wind was moving towards us, (this would be important as our scent wouldn't be blowing towards the bears) Doug knew we could get into a good position to watch the bears without them being able to detect our scent... positioning ourselves low to the ground and behind some alder bushes, ensured we would not be seen, but also enabled us to get a good view of the bears... there was one moment when the sow quickly stood up and looked right in our direction... her head was enormous... our eyes met... my heart began beating loudly... Doug warned me to stay low to the ground and be quiet... i hugged the ground remaining absolutely motionless and silent, sure the bear could hear my heart pounding away... after a minute, which seemed like an eternity, the sow settled back down and resumed eating some berries... meanwhile the cubs, tired from wrestling around with each other, curled up with one another for a nap... a decision was made that now would be a good time to quietly leave the area...

eventually we encountered a cold glacier stream that had to be crossed... its water, milky in color from the debris carried by the multitude of glaciers scouring the mountains (geologists called these sediments in the water, glacier flour, since the size of the sediments resemble baking flour) was carefully forded... our wet and muddy boots led us to a steep slope carpeted with a variety of subalpine vegetation and a scattering of rock outcrops... several of the outcrops were painted with a multitude of colors from lichen, formed into an abundance of abstract designs due to their incredible diversity... their names were impossible to learn, as first each species of lichen had to be identified before its name could be determined (there are over three thousand species of lichen just in North America)... as we looked towards the top of the slopes, a small herd of Dall Sheep were spotted grazing on the vegetation... would it be possible, but for a moment to enter their world... slowly the slope was climbed... i tried to climb this slope as fast as possible, but it became harder to breathe... sweat covered my face... the sheep were getting closer as more of the slope was below rather than above... but still onward i climbed, wanting to get close enough to sit and watch the sheep while trying to get some great photos... finally with the sheep close by and still unaffected from my presence, burst after burst of countless frames were taken in a desperate attempt to capture their essence... at times this task becomes impossible, and it's best just to put your camera down... i tried to absorb everything, the interplay between all the aspects of this natural world, the clouds, a gentle breeze, the sunlight, and the sheep... a cool breeze was felt while listening to the song of the wind in these hills... seeing and experiencing it with all my senses rather than just through the viewfinder of a camera... without the camera to restrict what you see and feel, it's easier to become a part of these hills in that moment... a oneness with all that surrounds you...

at times a person wants time to stand still, but sadly it's impossible... knowing i had intruded upon their world long enough it was time to leave them in peace... after bidding the sheep farewell, the long hike down the hills and towards the road was started... joining up again with Doug, we attempted to catch a ride on the next inbound bus.. our pace was slow as deep as in our hearts we knew this would be the last hike in Denali National Park and each of us wanted it never to end... after about an hour we approached the Park Road, but my eyes continually searched the hills while frantically trying to absorb every last bit of this paradise... and then it was over...

getting comfortable in my tent and protected from the mosquitoes, thoughts were written while they remained fresh... tomorrow we will sadly leave the park and continue our Alaskan journey...

Yuma Point, Grand Canyon

i must hold on to these thoughts… i must hold them so they will not be forgotten, and to do that, once again i take my pen into my hand…

before me another masterpiece is being painted while i sit and rest, colors change from shades of blues and grays to the reds and greens of mid-morning… i sit upon a rock, a pedestal that allows me to view this painting while the warmth of the early morning sun bathes my body… in my hand a mug of hot Tang to take the morning chill away… a friend sits close by but we sit in a treasured silence, each in our own thoughts, yet if we could listen out loud to these thoughts would not our prayers be similar… we both love this chasm the river created, and it doesn't matter how many times i walk within its depth, my love only grows… i stare down upon the muddy Colorado as it flows westward through this cathedral it has created… i look upon worlds that few have felt with the soles of their boots, only wishing i could give mine the chance… my thoughts wander to a trip i took down another part of this canyon, the magic in my father's eyes… his questions, a desire to grasp it all, to understand… yes, he too loved this world i hike within, and these memories are mine alone to hold and treasure, for it was i who led him into this rocky realm… i remember we talked some, but mostly listened to our own dreams and now years later we still are joined by this kingdom created by time… my father's ashes and his spirit are strong within these rocks… he is the wind, the river and the very heart and soul of this rocky paradise… i'll always remember that day i carried his ashes here, and i often wonder, who will carry mine… what thoughts will they carry, will their love for this National Park be as strong as mine… many hours have been spent listening to the rhythm of my steps and with this i have painted so many memories… i've seen the canyon's many moods, felt the cold rain and wind, and i've spent enough of my time cursing the warmth of the sun… and after all those miles i still feel i don't know this friend well enough… but will i ever…

i think of my life, so lucky i am, rich in the time spent walking in my boots with my shadow… i have viewed so many distant mountains that the others know not of, and i know i would not trade this wealth for anything… and i thank the lord for her that waits patiently for my boots to lead me home time and time again… she has given unto me so freely, and in all the miles that my boots have taken me, i've always carried her love within my heart… she is my canyon…

February 25, 1990

this morning i watched, in a silent reverence, the sun slowly bring a soft glow and warmth into this canyon… a light overcast of clouds softened the colors being painted on this canvas once again… a mug of hot Tang warmed my soul while my early morning thoughts became my silent prayers… my stomach has been satisfied with my bowl of warm oatmeal, so now i sit and reluctantly await my journey home… what thoughts i shall carry with me on this morning i know not, my mind will drift freely… the trail that led us to this point is still covered in snow so our empty footprints from two days past will be our silent guide as we follow them quietly into the upper parts of this snow covered canyon… it's in these final moments now, before i must leave, that i stand in silent prayer and try to paint my last memories of the majestic solitude that surrounded me in these past days… the canyon to the east is being bathed in colors of blues and dark greens while the inner gorge looks cold and forbidden as the river flows in silence onward through time… how many others will sit upon this rock… i wonder have others stood here before me as i do now… and of the future… the river is constant as it will flow through the epochs of time measured by these rocks… each of us will take a part of this peace to our other worlds in which we must exist... this trip has been good for my soul... i finished tying my boots, a task i've done countless times before, only to find myself restless to move on... my boots are still cold and await the warmth of my body... i know the time is at hand... my silent goodbyes are prayed and i take the first of many steps knowing in my heart this day will be good...

jtalarico

Bellingham Alaskan
Ferry Terminal

a year ago today i stood on the deck of the MV Columbia, an Alaskan Ferry, on my Alaskan adventure... today i was in Bellingham for the day and decided to watch the ferry depart for Alaska... what follows are my thoughts...

a bright pallet of colors against the pure white of the decks... the strong smell of salt saturates the air... casting my eyes upon the decks, i see the voyagers have already anchored their travel weary possessions into piles, and the piles form small colonies that will be their home, on this deck, for future days... the multi-assorted shapes of erected tents that will soon taste the salt of the sea decorate the decks... people of all sorts stand shoulder to shoulder along the ship's railings... the voyager with only his backpack is leaning on the railing and faithfully by his feet a worn jacket lays to shelter him in the days ahead... a family with a video camera capturing the last scenes of the first of an adventure... a young couple holding hands, their jackets look untested for the voyage ahead but they each wear a beautiful smile... was this their dream or even a honeymoon that is now unfolding... standing on this terminal dock i can not only sense but also feel their excitement... an excitement that forms a strong bond amongst these souls... conversation is flowing freely of distant ports in a far away land... i want to reach out and once again be part of this journey... your boots stand on the decks while mine have to stand with envy on this terminal dock... memories flood my mind with feelings i yearn to possess again... the ship's horn sounds and shatters the silence and causes a deep sense of despair as i know this voyage will not be mine for the taking... the excitement painted on their faces is undeniable, and i wish i could hear their joyful chatter... slowly the ferry shows the motion of departing...

i can remember a cold damp rain that fell as i too stood on a deck… i was on my Alaskan journey, and i watched continuously as the silhouettes of unknown shores drifted by… i too slept upon the deck with only my sleeping bag and a tarp to shelter me… i also had that excitement filling my soul, and out of all my memories, i miss that sense of excitement that lies deep within the heart of every voyager the most…

but now i stand on the dock with my thoughts as you drift slowly away… i bid you all clear skies and a smooth sea, the smell of salt that will rain upon you daily as the wind blows wildly through your hair… promise me you will stand guardian along the decks casting eyes upon the shoreline while it gradually changes from forests to mountains… and within days the glaciers will fill your skies while eagles, gulls, and ravens will look down upon you… ah, my travelers, go softly onto the sea and into your dreams… i bid you think not of me but of what lies ahead…

slowly i walk away with a tear and a longing in my heart…

jtalarico

July 7, 1990

Reflections from a Small Journey Lake
Union, WA
June 1990

Joanne had a certain glow in her eyes as i stood before the kayaks that laid deserted upon this wooden dock... she knew the excitement i was feeling, and was happy to give this moment to me... an innocence i felt, not wanting to stand out for my ignorance was plenty... i listened to the instructor...words of experience... then slowly and with awkward motions i wore the reflection of he who travels upon the sea... my kayak is gently placed upon the water... in the distance Joanne stands restless... she feels my excitement, for she knows my every mood, yet she is worried for my safety... my heart races as the kayak slowly drifts and leaves the security of the dock... the rhythm of my paddling is slow and awkward at first, yet i feel a oneness with the sea... so low i sit, as if i too was the waves upon the sea... the sounds of my paddles as they slowly put a distance between Joanne who waits... my mind races with excitement, for i want to totally encompass this moment...

now at times i'm sailing the straits to Alaska, or the rocky coast of Maine... my world fit securely within this vessel... to feel the rhythm of the sea, its tides, and its every mood... the salt within the air would fill my lungs... my hair wrapped warmly in a simple wool cap, protected from the damp and non-forgiving wind..., the penetrating coldness of the air surrounds my every move... my muscles work without thought in a fluid of movements that sends a lonely warmth to my soul... i feel the mystery and power of the sea as i attempt to defy its mind and proceed to unknown points guided by the needle of a trusty compass... my senses always alert for the changing of her ways... the fury that an ocean wind can carry...

onward i paddle as the haunting cries of the gulls accompany my lonely thoughts...

my thoughts take me back to the present... i look up, Joanne sits upon the dock, patiently waiting, filled with a happiness as she watches my movements... with my harbor in sight, i slowly turn my craft against the wind and voyage homeward... my kayak feels the security of its mooring... my journey is over... as i walk away i promise myself to feel the sea again, another journey, another time...

The Passing of a Distant Storm

on an alpine saddle beside Yellow Astor Butte, North Cascades…

on this journey my boots had taken me to the multitude of alpine lakes, valleys and mountains that form part of the North Cascades… several days into my hike i was camped on a distant mountain with a beautiful view in every direction when this storm passed by…

a distant rumbling of thunder breaks the silence of the early evening… a cool evening breeze stirs and takes away the heat from the late afternoon… i sit by my tent, a mug of hot tea warms my hands while my wool cap is bringing comfort to my ears… to my west Mt. Shuskan… alpine glaciers and the remnants of late winter snows still dress its ragged peaks… solitary mountains, in every direction, fill my horizons… their names still unknown… as evening approaches, lonely shades of blues and grays are painting the mountain skies… the steel blue clouds that quickly march in are easing a distant mountain's grayish blue silhouette… curtains of rain silently drift through the mountains… i watch as far off mountain peaks are silently fading away only to reappear as the distant storm passes… bolts of lightning fill the sky around me… cracks of thunder shatter the silence… automatically i count the seconds and calculate its distance… the wind carries the refreshing smell of a late summer rain and it encircles my world awakening my senses… the temperature of the air drops rapidly… i want to pull out my rain gear as this storm approaches but i hesitate in order to watch this spectacle as it unfolding before me… the sky to my east, once a pale and faded blue is slowly turning to a lonely gray as the fingers of the storm steal away its cloudless sky… to the west the steel gray clouds thin quietly allowing painted streaks of a faded red to tell of a now distant sunset… the air around me becomes cooler as heavy drops of rain fall… fingers of this passing storm… i retreat to my tent, sheltering me from the rain… the wind blows fiercely… my tent walls rattled by the winds but hold strong… then all is silent and motionless… the rains stop… as i leave my tent the distant eastern mountains are now cleansed by the rains and a blue cloudless sky paints the silhouettes of these distant peaks… faint streaks of red are slowly fading into a purple… i sit alone and watch this passing of a distant storm…

jtalarico
July 11, 1990

Preface to "the assent"

one accumulates many dreams within a lifetime... some of our dreams we silently wonder if we will ever be able to make them a part of our memory of moments that mark our passage within this carousal called life... recently i had taken up rock climbing to further enhance my experience within this world of mountains and canyons that i have come to love... but in all my years of walking with my boots i have always looked upward to that world of ice and snow that carpets the mountain summits that i have come to love... what would it be like to have my boots take me into that world... i loved reading the stories of those that climbed Annapurna, Everest and K2, always secretly wondering not only would i, but more importantly, could i ever master the skills to walk within this world... as with every dream one must begin with baby steps and my first steps towards this dream was attending a week-long course on alpine mountaineering that ended with a summit bid on Mt. Baker in Washington... what follows was the summit entry taken from my journal as my week long course ended...

"the ascent"
it is 7:30 at night yet the sun still sits with an hour and half of light to bestow upon us before we will witness another mountain sunset... within our tent, upon a river of ice, i sit... my face and ears feeling the wrath of the sun... tender to the touch, so once again i apply my mountain paint (zinc oxide) to ease the pain... my body must sleep now for in a few hours i must rise to climb my mountain... i lie awaiting sleep but once again my thoughts are the pages of knowledge that i have danced to these past few days... my sleep is interrupted and within an hour i rise to once again do my

nightly ritual upon the snow… now alone on this sea of ice i scan my horizons, behind me silently stands my mountain waiting… i cast my eyes towards the sea as the golden shadows of evening are beginning to appear… Mt. Rainier, Glacier Peak and the Sisters all stand as silent guardians to this world of ice and snow that i now stand gently on… i want to stand here and watch night silently creep over this world of which i am a part, but i am cold and i must sleep… i must stay warm, save my energy for the hours ahead… i find the warmth of my sleeping bag but once again my mind is far from sleep, so i let my thoughts drift through emotions and visions from the past days of living on this mountain… always feeling the presence of the mountain… in and out of sleep i pass the hours until we hear the sounds to prepare…

slowly i leave the security of my warm sleeping bag… the cold air of the early morning 2:00 a.m. chills my body until i quickly find my shirt, pants and jacket… without any thought i light my stove, a ritual i have preform countless times and even though my the hand motions are awkward my stove comes alive… i soon feel the warmth of the stove… slowly i prepare my food that will not only warm my body but provide me the energy i will need throughout this morning… my oatmeal, honey and hot chocolate sends a welcoming warmth thru my body… i dress now for my summit climb and, in this moment of time, it seems like i waited an eternity for this day… now with the learned movements of my week long course i dress to the reflection of a climber… i stand in the darkness of a day that has yet to dawn… i stand in reverence and i stand alone in prayer… the sky is painted with countless stars while the milky way forms a celestial ribbon that spirals downward towards the sea… in the distance the lights of far away cities shine silently as i look down on a world that seems so far removed from this cold world of ice and snow that i stand upon… behind me stands the my mountain in all its beauty… the snows that carpet its summit appears a soft white… the mountain's silhouette paints a gentle picture to the eyes hiding the steepness of its slopes that soon my legs must climb… in this moment of silence i find a sense of peace with all that surrounds me… now as i stand with my climbing partner, i check and recheck my harness… the tugging on knots that are now tied from memory… slowly i gasp the rope that will unite us all and tie upon this line… still more knots are tied as i go through the ritual of preparation… each of us now will check one other… my heart races with excitement as we all slowly position ourselves to begin our climb… my headlamp casts a false light upon the snow, a light that i shall follow through the early hours of dawn… the word "ready" is heard as slowly i begin to cast my evening shadow unto this mountain and let my boots take their first steps…

slowly we begin… my hands now grasping my ice ax, move in a repetition of learned movements, movements that will slowly and safely take me towards my summit… i follow the footsteps of our mountain guide who has walked upon many a mountains… i wonder what it must be like to walk in his boots… are his thoughts of this mountain summit or summits far away to which his boots have yet to take him to… often we hear our guide's words reaffirming to me that his mind is on the task he must now do, take us safely towards this summit… my thoughts are slow to wander as i must concentrate on the task before me… step after step, breath follows breath as the evening chill quickly leaves my body… my body becomes embraced in a warmth from this slow dance i now perform as we slowly move upwards… the hours pass by… i remember only the repeated motions of my steps and the muscles becoming tired as they move me upwards… at times i would lift my head upward wondering have we made any progress at all… always the mountain slopes upward… behind me i can see the reflections of all my steps… the beating of my heart and the rhythm of my breathing is all that i feel at times, yet at other times i think of the reality of what i am doing, i am finally living within the world that i dreamed about so often and it matters not that this is just a small summit in the north Cascades and not a far away Himalayan mountain, for i am climbing… i pray in thanks often as slowly my feet dance the motions of a climber… i try to think not of the steepness or how tired i am becoming… i will often cast my eyes upon my boots… my crampons cast upon the ice… i trust their touch upon the ice as slowly my repeated steps turn into minutes and hours… my world is now lit by the fading darkness of night, dawn is awakening… the odor of sulfur fills the air, evidence of the breathing of this sleeping mountain… upwards it spills its steam into the heavens as from this lower crater we now must climb… all i can know is the tiredness of my body… no real thoughts can but only the constant prayers for the strength i need as my legs slowly respond time and time again… at times i cast my eyes upon this scene from above as i see the reflection of a climber and i realized that this climber is me… i am flooded with emotions that cast my weariness aside and pushed me onward… dreams became reality… always my departed father's presence is felt as i walked at times for the two of us… i asked if this is a false summit that looms above me… still higher i must climb, and now the first rays of the new day's light colors our world in the most beautiful way… the shadow of this mountain is cast for miles unto the mountains below as the snow upon these peaks glows a virgin whiteness… the rebirth of another day… onward and onward until there within my sight appears the summit… slowly we approached… i am over whelmed with the presence of my father… i felt his hand upon mine as we walked onward… the tears slowly cascading into my sweat as my thoughts become only of him, and as i slowly walked unto the summit i cried silently for us both, for this dream and for Joanne…

i couldn't talk as my emotions were overwhelming me… as i looked upon the mountain peaks below, dressed in the morning dawn i prayed silently in thanks… now upon this peak we all stood… the pictures will recall the minutes as i was congratulated by our guide… i don't think he will ever know the thanks i felt at that moment… to him another peak, to me, well he helped me paint my wildest dream… as the coldness of the dawn chilled my body, i cast my eyes upon the beauty that was before me... over and over silently i cried in joy... on a summit in the north cascades, lies a mountain register... within this box is a worn notebook filled with thoughts of they who came before me... somewhere within the filled pages an empty space was found... "this one was for you dad July 20, 1990"

my emotions revealed the secrets of why i guess one climbs upon these peaks... and to you Matt... in thanks, for your friendship... i wish for you the highest peaks...

jtalarico

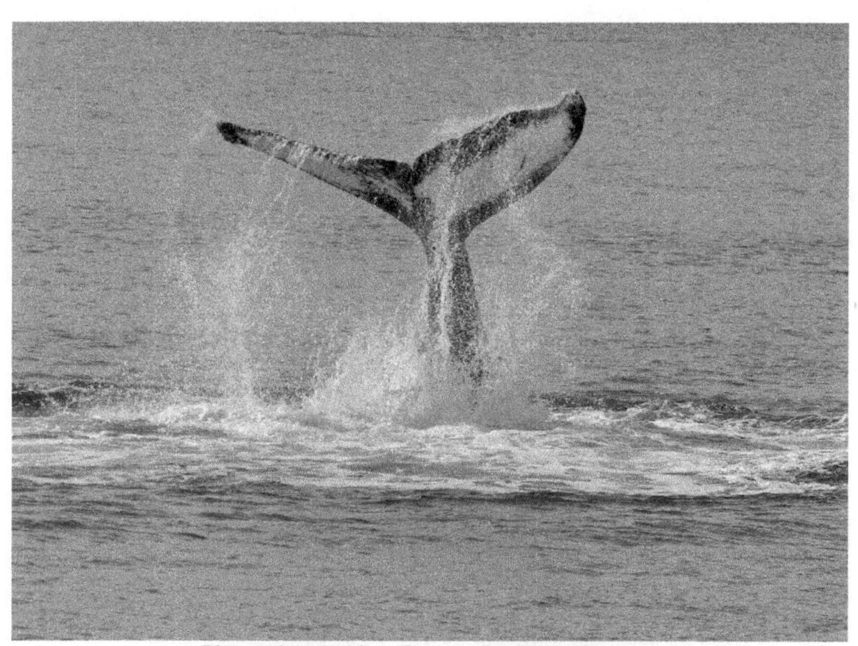

Flame showing her fluke Aoke Bay, Alaska

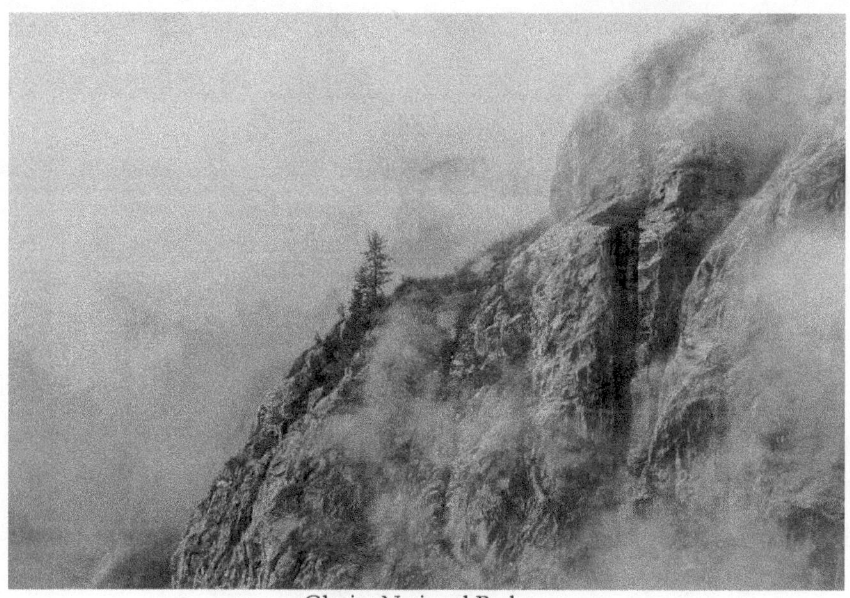

Glacier National Park

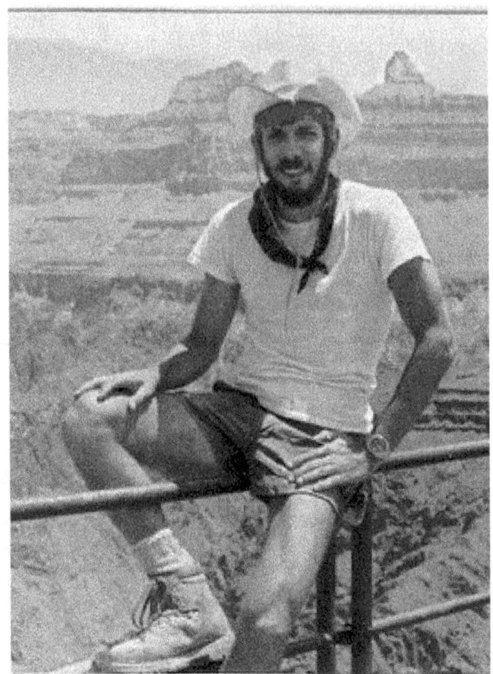

Grand Canyon 1977

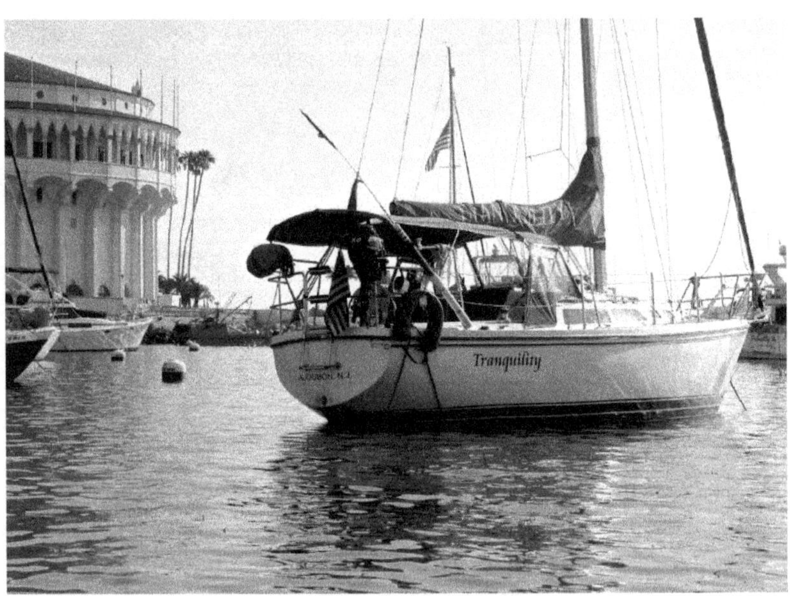

Tranquility mooring in Catalina

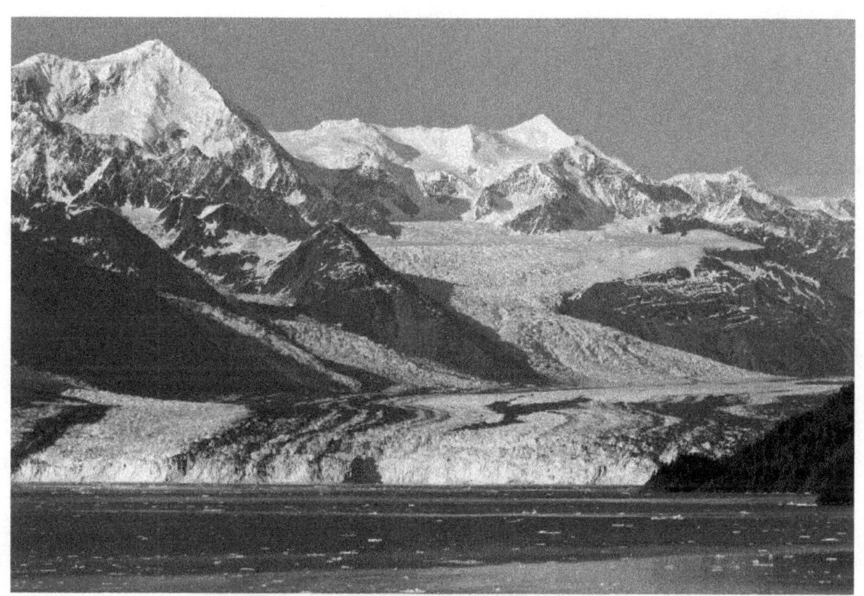

Harvard Glacier, College Fjord, Alaska

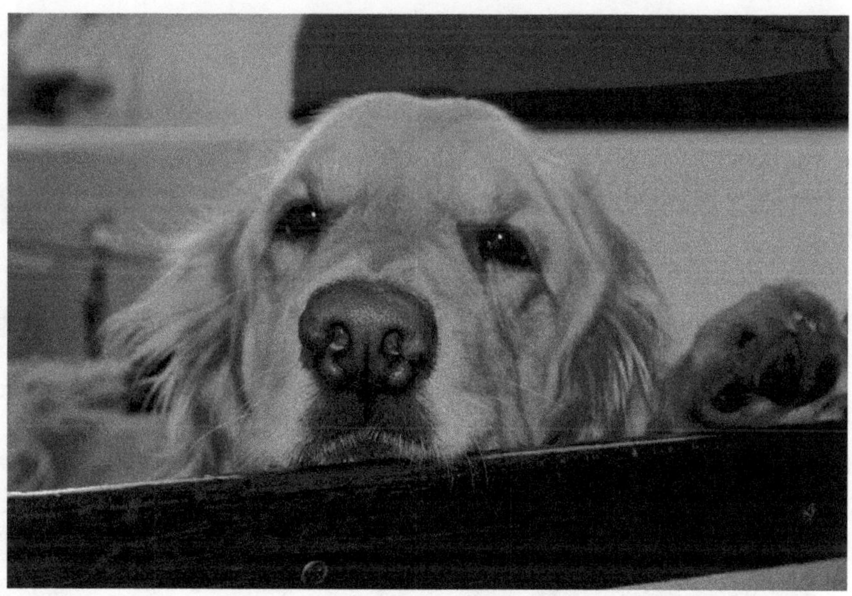

Joshua

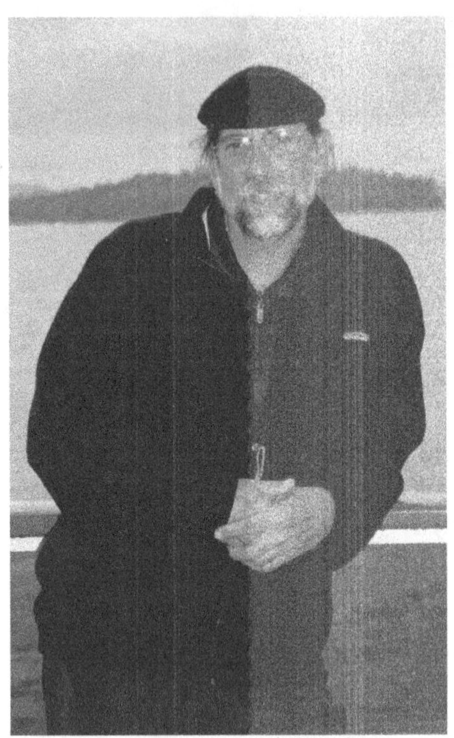

Aboard The Ruby Princess 2016

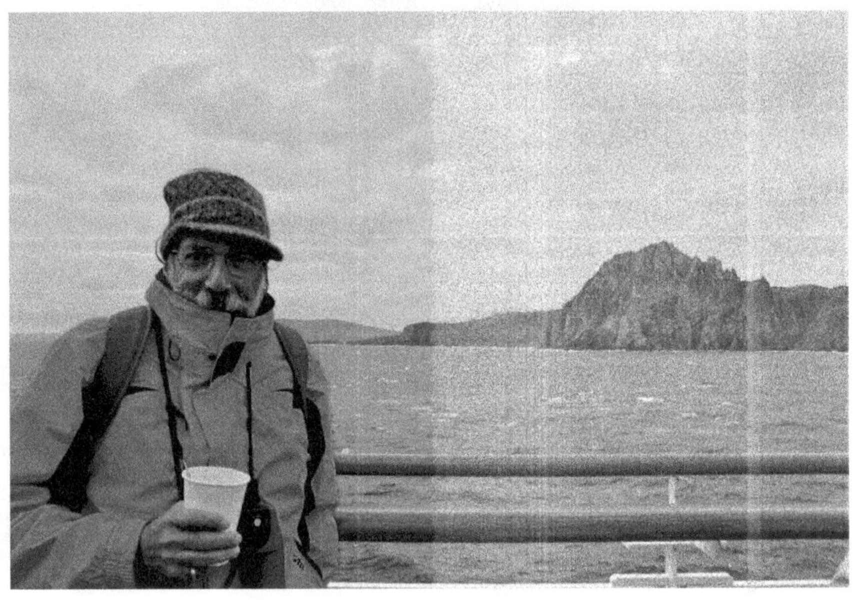

Rounding Cape Horn on the Star Pincess

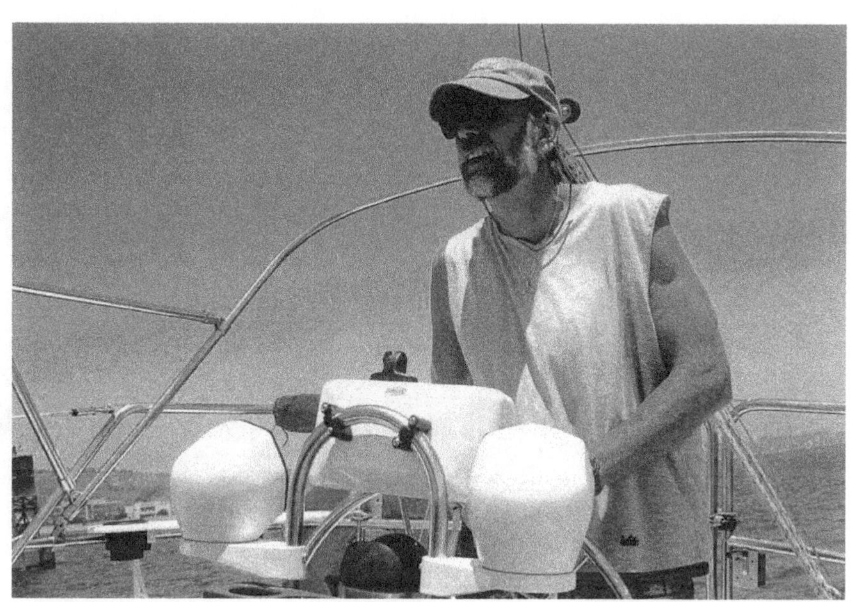

Sailing Tranquility

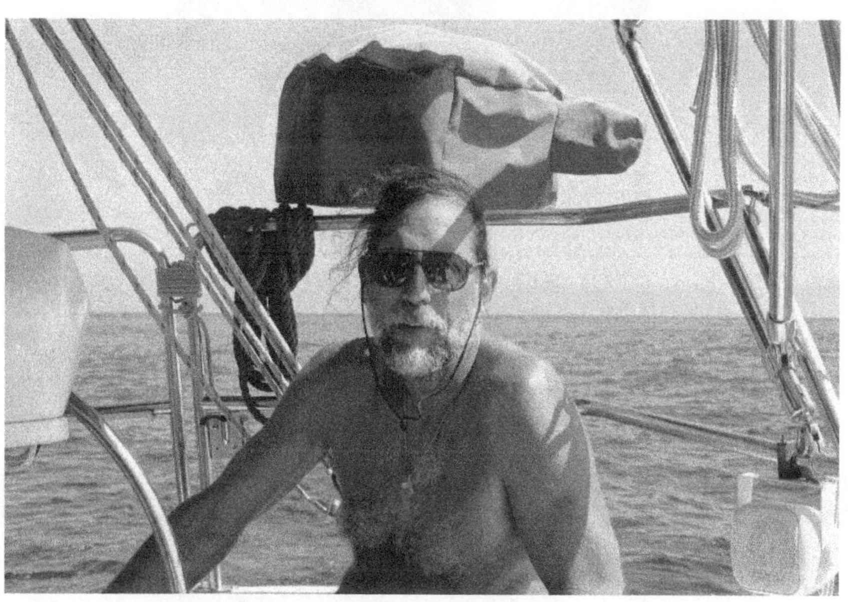

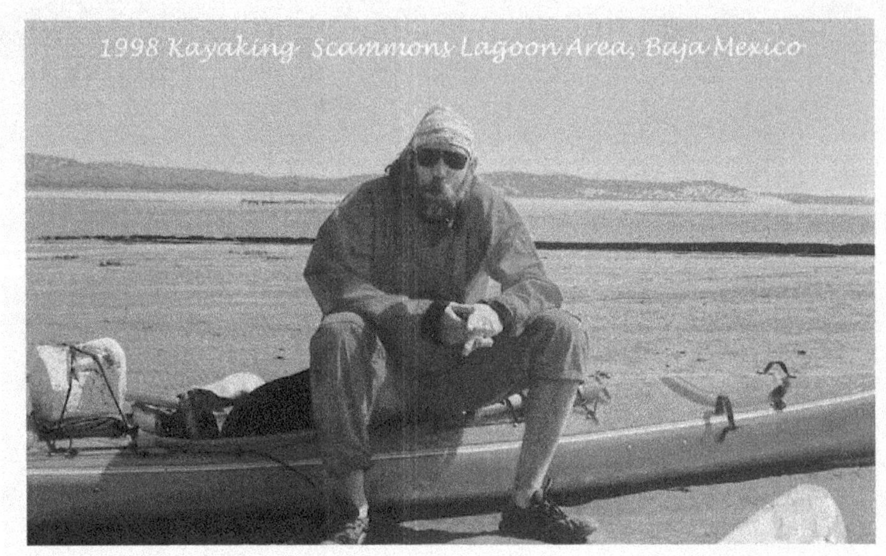

Kayaking

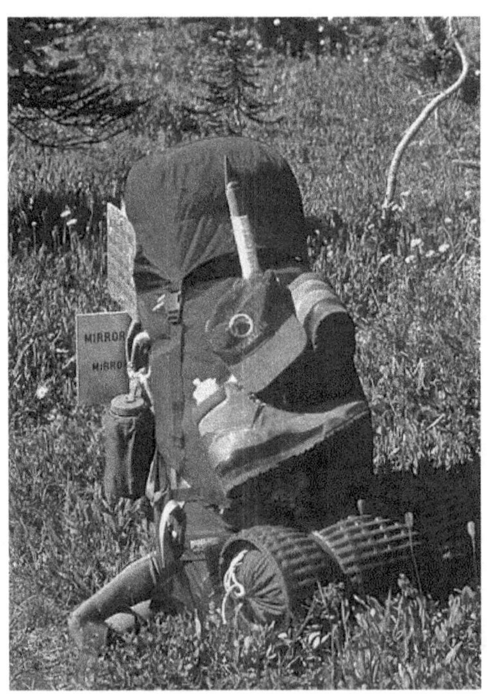

Backpack at Mt. Rainer's Wonderland Trail

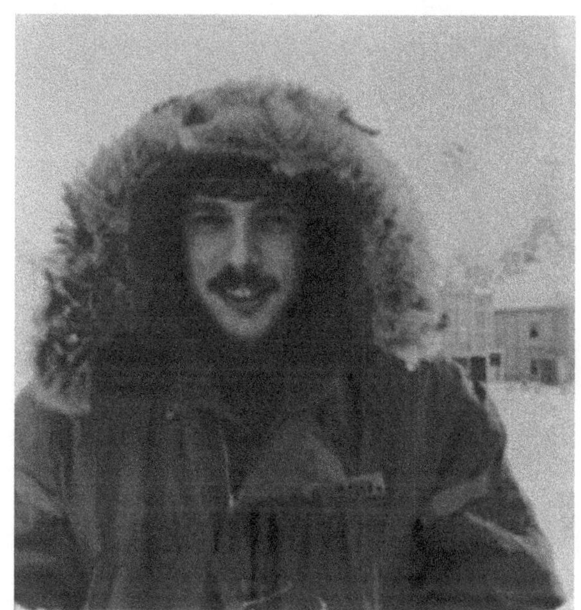

Greenland 1975

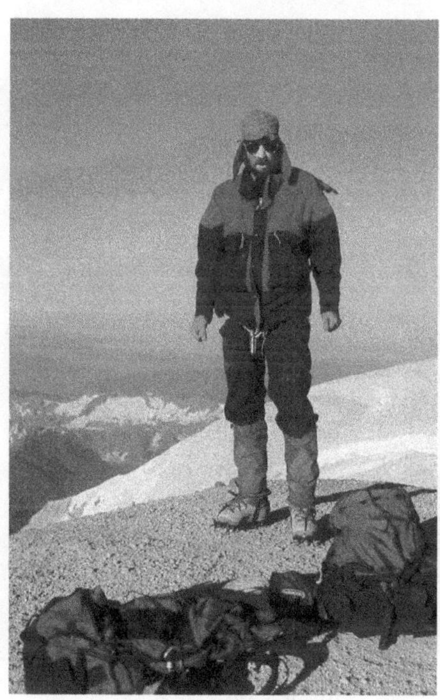

Summit of Mt. Baker

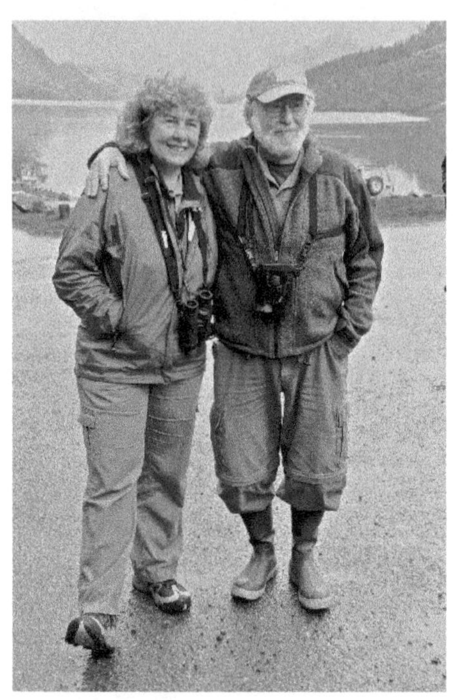

Two great friends Judy and John who taught me about the Tongass Forest

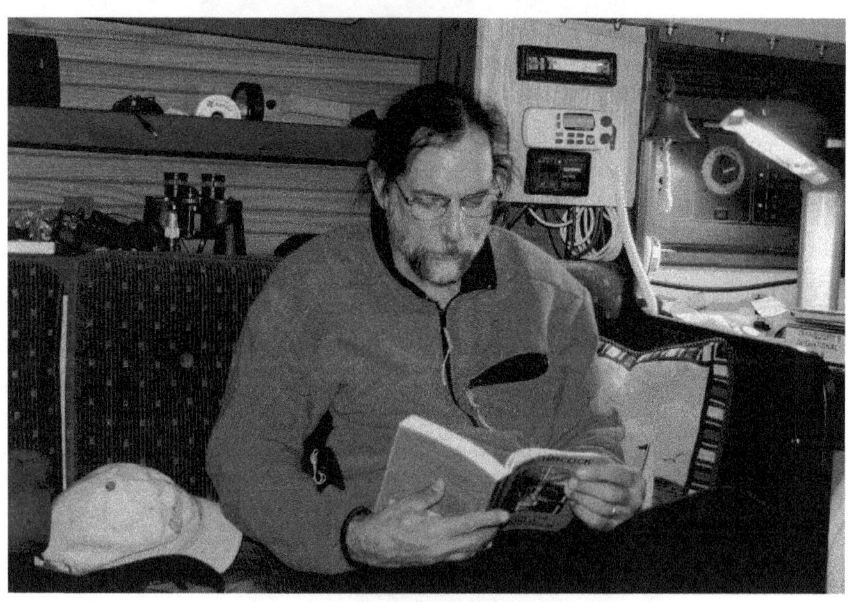

Reading on Tranquility

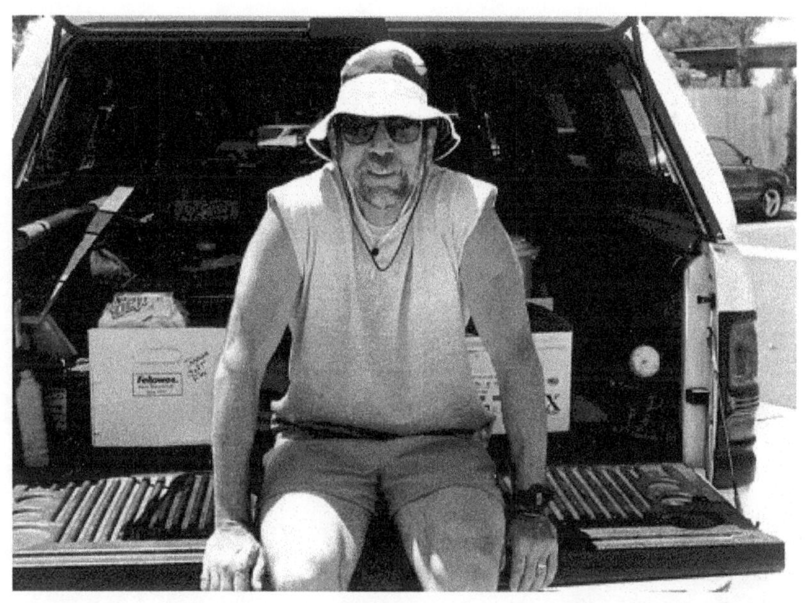

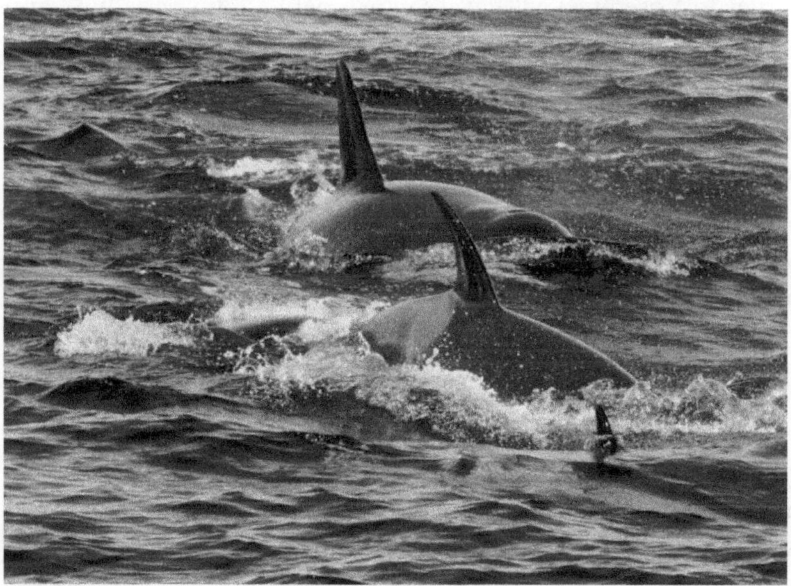

Orcas in the San Juan Islands

Yosemite Days
Summer 1991

i wish i could remember when i first spoke John Muir's name or picked up a book filled with his words, but i can't… i know though that Muir's words touched my soul and changed my thinking, and in the end i slowly became a disciple of his teachings…slowly his books filled my shelves and i read and reread these books… pages gently worn from my fingers caressing them… i took his words deep into my heart, and as the years passed i became very curious about Muir's special place, Yosemite… the more i read about Yosemite, and the more John Muir spoke of his deep love for Yosemite, i knew i would eventually have to experience his world for myself… my first journey to Yosemite i will always remember… it was early June, and there was still snow in the high country… i had planned a trip, all school year long, to spend several weeks hiking alone in the backcountry of Yosemite… first i would spend several days in Yosemite Valley with its sheer walls of granite that i knew would hold me in a dream-like world… after a few weeks in the backcountry, i would head down to Yosemite Valley once again to spend a day before i journeyed home…

June 2, 1991

written in Lone Pine Campground

once again i find myself with pen in hand and a head full of thoughts… today marks the first day of my summer vacation, yet i am filled with mixed feelings for i find myself now hundreds of miles away from Joanne… my garden is at the foot of Mt. Whitney, the tallest mountain in the continental United States and heart of the high Sierras… it's these mountains, the Sierra Nevada, that form the barrier between the sea that i love and the eastern foothills that i now travel along… i love the mountains, but i also love the sea …

now i must have patience, for my love of the sea must wait until i have quenched my thirst for the mountains that have also captured my soul...

my moments now are here... here amongst these walls of granite... whitish grey in color, these rocks form spirals, like those of a cathedral that point upwards towards the heavens... a mystical yearning always draws my eyes upward, upward towards the distant peaks... at times i study these rocks from different perspectives, be it with the eyes of a geologist who can unravel the stories the rocks have to tell, while at other times, with the heart of one who wishes to dance upon their surface... what a magical touch one must have to be a rock climber... to dance a ballet upon these stages... walls so steep and majestic... feeling so humble... i sing my praises to their essence...

to the east are the Alabama Hills, an interesting outcrop of jointed rock... thoughts of Pinnacle Peak back in Arizona that now lies far from my eyes... but these monuments of stone are on a much grander scale... what hidden stories these rocks must hold... tonight my garden is the high desert, creosote-like bushes scattered about, yet the bright green of cottonwoods outline the path of a stream ... the weathered sands from mountains makes up my carpet, the carpet upon which my tent is pitched... enormous boulders lie scattered about, left behind from the passing days when glaciers formed this parcel of heaven... many of these rocks yearn for the chalked hands of a climber to dance on their stage of rock... i want to spend hours bouldering, in this paradise, but my knees are fragile and hurt, and i know i must save them for the days ahead... the voice of a ranger, just days ago, told me of what to expect in the high backcountry of Yosemite... a world filled with snow and ice bound lakes that may shorten or reroute my planned hike... if that be the case, i can accept that fate as i know i will return once again in late summer... hopefully my troubled knee holds out this summer as even now i wait to hear from yet another orthopedic doctor regarding possible knee surgery… i placed my tent with its door to the west in hopes that in the early hours of a new day i might witness an alpenglow on the eastern escarpment of these majestic mountains… already the air begins to cool down as the dawn of this ending day silently approaches…

i find myself still unsettled within my garden of rock… mixed feelings as to where i am and all that i left behind… the end of this school year came quickly and with tragedy as we lost one of our wrestlers from the team i helped coached… Chad, our state champion for this past wrestling season will be missed in so many ways, and i am so unsettled at what took him at such a young age… he was so strong and defiant, yet so fragile…

just yesterday my thoughts raced back and forth on taking this trip, proof of my unsettled spirit… i felt the magic from last summer, a summer in which i first witnessed the world of Yosemite, and it was these feelings that convinced me to return once again… all i did last summer was to briefly pass through Yosemite in one of many days of travel that took us throughout California… this summer i planned to experience Yosemite intimately as Muir would have wanted… as i left home, i left without the excitement that filled my soul last summer, but as the miles slowly passed, i felt the mountains spinning their spell and drawing the excitement from my soul…

my jeep ran well today as the miles slowly passed… tires beating out the rhythm of the highway… music filling my world… even though i made good time today i stopped often to paint a memory with my camera, memories that i regretted i didn't take last summer…

i remembered with every journey one takes, one must have patience in finding a rhythm, and in my heart i believed with the passing miles that rhythm and dance would eventually come as naturally as ever…

my mixed feelings in leaving were apparent as i had not prepared a meal for tonight...

i didn't want to start to take food from my caches that would be needed later, so i simply made some tea knowing that i could stop for breakfast in the little mountain town of Bishop... Joanne and i fell in love with that little town last year, a gateway into the backcountry of the Sierras, and they had great pancakes!

as the evening settled in, a small camper, much like ours, was set up not too far away from my campsite, and with that came thoughts of Joanne's and my summer soon to be... two vagabonds stealing memories throughout our summer journey...

June 3, 1991
written in Yosemite's Climbers Campground, reflecting on my second day of travel

i awoke early... all was quiet with the sun about five minutes from its dawning for yet another day... the sky was clean and crystal clear, a far cry from the daily smog blanketing Phoenix...i grabbed my camera and walked a short way up the Whitney Portal Trail to await the warmth of the sun shining upon these distant summits... even though a faint touch of pink, from the early morning sun, never dressed these cliffs their reflection stood bold against the early dawn sky... my camera clicked away as images were recorded... from my many travels i've learned that nature always paints a canvas that is a masterpiece... returning to my little camp i quickly heated up my cup of Tang that warmed my soul for the tasks at hand... slowly i began my ritual of tearing down my little campsite and packing up... soon i was once again happily heading down a highway... the low eastern position of the rising sun lighted the rocks of the Alabama Hills with a dramatic signature and had me stop, time and time again, to paint yet another reflection with my camera... as i drove northward the beauty of these snow covered peaks guided me to the little mountain town of Bishop... a hot breakfast of pancakes fueled me through the remaining miles of my drive along the eastern escarpment of the Sierras… thoughts drifted endlessly as my eyes witnessed the silent beauty of these peaks… summits covered with a winter's snow stood boldly against the early morning sky painted in pastels of blue… slowly i watched the geology change as evidence of a world of volcanism now appeared… soon i would be passing an area known for its basaltic columns, the Devil's Post Pile, a must for geologists to visit, but my sense of urgency told my spirit that it must wait for another journey to allow my boots to walk that trail… i was becoming more and more excited as i could feel the mountains screaming to my spirit… my music played louder as it filled my spirit with the joy that only music can… a mountain high was pulsating through my soul now… the image of Mono Lake told me that very soon i would head westward over these summits to my world of Yosemite… so with the morning sun on my back, i slowly began a climb into yet another world, a world i would never regret entering… with my spirit racing and my eyes dancing over this landscape, my heart knew i was finally bound for Yosemite… the Tioga Pass road climbed steadily upward and this world became one of sheer cliffs and snow… higher and higher the road climbed into the mountains… i could only imagine what beauty awaited my eyes… after paying my entrance fee, and having a brief conversation with the park ranger, i put my jeep into gear and entered Yosemite… the music within my soul beat a soulful rhythm as my radio screamed out the song "Carry On" by CSN… i love this song and sang along with the excitement of a small child… the world of Yosemite was so beautiful, and i cried for as a poet i knew not the combinations of words or the colors an artist would paint to express my true feelings… onward i drove through a world that was slowly awakening from its winter sleep… lakes still frozen and a blanket of snow delayed the arrival of spring into this world… finally entering the valley of Yosemite i was greeted by its vertical cliffs that protected and formed this valley… i cried because i knew not the ballet to dance upon these polished rocks of granite… i could only pray that someday my chalked hands would touch these monuments of stone… eventually i entered Yosemite Valley and received a permit for the walk-in campground, a campground reserved for the rock climbers… i picked this campground as i did not want to be among the hundreds of tourists with their noisy tv's and generators… tourists who came with a heart and intentions not like mine… looking for a vacant spot, i walked quietly among the climbers as they organized their hardware for their next day's climb… innocently i would stop to watch, only wishing i had their skill to climb… my hands and feet were restless to learn this ballet on the rocks… after claiming my camping spot and without the magic of Joanne's hand in mine, i walked the few little shops looking for some food… i bought a sandwich and then drove to an empty viewpoint and ate quietly while watching the distant climbers on El Capitan… by the trailhead leading to El Capitan a small crowd gathered to watch a fallen climber be attended to… the reality of gravity… a fallen climber lying on a backboard with a neck-brace as he awaited further transportation… i learned that this was only one of several falls in the past few days…

later that night, with a hot mug of Tang and sitting outside my tent, i ended my first day in Yosemite with thoughts of the days ahead and always a prayer for Joanne… i love you Joanne for letting me have my world of dreams…

June 4, 1991
Little Yosemite Campground

today was a day filled with a chaotic mix of emotions ranging from my mountain highs to the frustration of an disorganized departure and a poor night of sleep… i spent a restless night doing what seems like my ever-constant half hour repositioning rolls as i am never able to get comfortable or find the rhythm of a peaceful sleep… i realize that finding this rhythm will take several days as i slowly let the mountains sink into my soul… i awoke this morning and attempted to prepare my breakfast only to realize i didn't pack my little frying pan… the consequences of not having my frying pan means my breakfasts of pancakes, bread, and cinnamon rolls are a thing of the past… luckily i always bring my oatmeal, and i know that will help warm my bones in the early morning hours… but now as a consequence, i will have this extra weight of all my pancake mixes to carry throughout my trip, and weight is always a concern…

i arrived at Little Yosemite Campground in the early afternoon… after pitching my tent and making camp, i took a short hike with another hiker i met… Austin and i had a nice afternoon hike up to the base of Half Dome, and in doing so i was able to see this backcountry open up before my eyes… hypnotically i traced the sharp slope of the backside of Half Dome as it arched endlessly upward towards a hidden summit… a chain ladder was bolted to its sheer face to allow those who dare a climb to its summit… i held that chain securely in my hand, wanting so badly to climb that ladder, but knowing in my heart that the extreme exposure of height in that climb would be beyond what i could handle… conquering my fear of height is an ever constant battle for me in rock climbing, but still i wanted so badly to take that first big step… later in the day, as i stood in silence at an isolated viewpoint that overlooked Yosemite Valley far below, i admired Muir's world of Yosemite and began to understand why i had come… Mt. Hoffman and the Cathedral Range framed this canvas, and with every turn of my head a beautiful waterfall was witnessed cascading down from these granite walls… sadly the distant sound of their thunder was unable to find my ears… throughout that afternoon i constantly felt the calling of Half Dome, and at times i almost forgot my fears and thought that yes, i should have climbed that chain ladder… i knew though that i had to worry about my knee as climbing down would really stress it, and i still had to favor that knee as much as i could in the coming days of hard hiking…

my intentions were to continue along the Merced River and eventually make it up to a high sierra camp on Lake Merced which would mean about a thousand foot climb… i knew with a steady, slow pace i should have no problems even though i was carrying a heavy pack… if worse came to worst, my topographic map showed me there a cascade about half way to my destination with a flatten shelf that could possibly make for a nice stopping place for the night if i had to… i made a note to talk with a Ranger later that day…

(later)

after talking to the Ranger i decided to go directly to the lake in the morning… in my heart i knew the elevation gain could be no worse than the switchbacks on the South Kaibab trail in the Grand Canyon… just prior to sunset, Austin and i took a hike down to Nevada Falls… exploring around the thundering waters we found a beautiful hidden indentation in the rocks right behind the deafening cataract where we could watch and feel the water thundering over the rock… carefully we positioned ourselves in this small cavity… the power of that water was a frightful yet humbling experience and i could just imagine Muir trying to get ever so much closer to the cascading waters… for me, i was content right where i stood as i was held spellbound by its magic and power… as evening began to descend on the backcountry, both Austin and i wandered backed to our tents in a silence that we both enjoyed… i told Austin my plans for the next day and will wait to see if his boots will join mine…

June 5, 1991
Merced Lake

this morning i awoke and automatically fired up my stove, heated my water for my hot Tang… a ritual that i would repeat daily for the rest of my time in Yosemite… i saw that Austin's tent was gone and figured he was off doing the John Muir Trail as he mentioned yesterday… with silent thoughts of my awaiting day, i broke down my tent and hung it in hopes of catching the early sun and dry the night's dew… with all my gear now lying in an disorganized pile, i slowly began to place each item in its designated place in my backpack… years of enacting this ritual made my task easier as each item always has its own place… slowly my backpack filled.. i stuffed my dry tent into its dry bag, strapped it on my pack, and finally got my day's snacks placed where i would easily be able to get them during my various breaks… with Austin now gone, i would stick to my original plan even though i was still a little concerned about the 8.5 miles i would hike with a consistent elevation gain and carrying a heavy pack along(a heavy pack for me was always between 45 to 55 pounds which was somewhere around a third of my overall body weight… the typical recommendation is to carry about 20% of your body weight which, for me, would mean carrying around a 40 pound backpack)… my back felt good and my knees strong after yesterday's hike, but i still wanted to take it easy for the first few days…

the first two miles of my hike were a lovely walk in a forest laced with sugar pines and white fir and occasional glances of the steep cliffs of Yosemite… often i would stop to pick up a pine cone of a sugar pine and marvel at its size, being roughly about a foot long while the tallest trees on earth, the giant redwood, had a pine cone the size of my thumbnail… following the waters of the Merced River i kept a steady pace as the walk was fairly easy… at Bunnell Point my window to this paradise opened and the river transformed into numerous cascades that became my shadow as i gradually gained in elevation… for the next four miles my eyes feasted on the beauty of this backcountry… this was truly what i envisioned Yosemite to be like, magnificent granite domes filled my every view while the waters of the Merced led me steadily upward… i can't count the times i had to stop, for with every turn of the trail the canvas before me just got more beautiful… often i would stop just to scream out a prayer of praise for this cathedral i was hiking within; truly this was a garden of creation… even though my pack was heavy, my shoulders and knee actually felt pretty good… i stopped for my lunch perched on a throne overlooking this world carved out by the glaciers from an ancient past… i sat on the cool granite outcrop, its surface polished from years of the Merced overflowing… the noon sun felt good as i took off my shirt, soaked with a honest sweat, to dry… after a lunch of jerky and cheese, i continued my gradual climb to my awaiting destination… with each step my boots took, i slipped into the world of Yosemite and a wilderness that i had only imagined could exist… opened before me was the magic that i would learn Yosemite gave to Muir… seeing all this made the many words i read of Muir come true… i believed, at that moment, that the trail was the most beautiful trail my boots had ever taken me on, but how many times, in my past, have i echoed these very words… at one point i stopped only because i was spellbound by the simple enchantment of the Merced… i sat in silence while just feet away from me the power and fury of its meltwaters filled my world as the river exploded downward through canyon after canyon…

finally dragging my tired feet, i entered the area of Merced Lake… i must admit though, i was a little disappointed as this area was not as dramatic as the Enchanted Lakes of Washington which i had experienced the previous summer, but i knew in my heart i would still find the hidden beauty of this lake… slowly i began the never-ending task of breaking open my backpack and setting up camp… then to my surprise, out of the woods, into my camp walked Austin… Joanne is always happier when she knows i'm with somebody else, but i realized he and i both just wanted the solitude of a day's hike…

later that night a small but friendly Indian fire (a Native American seemed always to build a fire no larger than was necessary to meet his immediate needs… it was the White man that always had to build a fire bigger and bigger) provided a sense of warmth that enhanced and wrapped the companionship of strangers, sharing a campsite our boots took us to, and now a small fire… their only link, being united in that they all walked a trail ending here… we sat, sometimes in a silence that we held sacred… slowly the evening passed… often the silence would be broken as someone would tell of their travels… we would listen in reverence to their magical tales and then add our own… this is what i love about the magic of a campfire… always its warmth embraces you only to cast beautiful memories by the fire's end… each of us used these moments to help us search and define our inner peace, a peace that came unto us because of the beauty of Yosemite… this beauty becomes a part of our prayers and hymns that we always hold within our soul during this journey… silently the sky grew dark and a sea of stars could be seen… i shall sleep well tonight… tomorrow i will hike up to Washburn Lake and then hopefully into the Volgesang…

June 6, 1991

Lake Merced

with a constant gain in elevation, night time temperature dropped rapidly, as the cold mountain air enveloped the valley that Merced Lake sat within, blessing me with a good night's sleep… i slept so much better, partly due to the cold air that became my blanket, but also because my body slowly settled into its backcountry rhythm… the mountains had finally grabbed ahold of my soul and brought me a restful peace…

wrapped in the warmth of my sleeping bag, with no miles waiting to be hiked, i allowed myself to sleep later in the morning… i slowly rose around 7:30, but even at that hour i was still unable to feel the warmth of the morning sun due to the high peaks that surrounded Merced Lake… slowly i dressed and found my way to my trusty stove and fired it up… this is a ritual i have done countless times in my mountain journeys and soon the warmth of my mug of Tang filled my body and kept me warm until the warmth of the morning sun made its presence felt… after my bowl of oatmeal, i began to prepare for a day hike up to the snow fields around Babcock Lake… one of the purposes of this hike was to practice doing self-arrest and other techniques that i learned with my ice ax last summer… with Austin now sharing the trail, conversation accompanied our boots up towards the lake… progress was now slower as there was no need to put so many miles behind us… today we had the luxury to take countless breaks only to marvel at the world we were becoming absorbed into… gradually we rose above the canopy of this forest and the world of Yosemite came alive to us once again… this masterpiece was painted with endless mountains still locked in their winter snows… they looked so forbidding, yet in a way i could hear the mountain calling for my soul.. throughout the morning our boots kept us in a world of waterfalls with chaotic displays of the cascading waters of the Merced River… the night before, around our campfire, i learned that the river hasn't flowed this strong in many years… i feel blessed that i am witnessing this now… i wonder, did Muir see the Merced like this… and all i can hope is that this beauty is etched deep into my memories, a masterpiece, always to enjoy… gray cliffs of rock chiseled and sculpted by glaciers from an ice age long passed… trees, few but scattered amidst these sentinels of rock… at times all i can do is stop and give my prayers of thanks… i wonder have the words of a poet been written yet to let my soul really express this beauty… i read Muir's words often and now feel i can finally understand what he felt living in his garden of Yosemite… do i also have the eyes of Muir, i wonder yet hope for this gift also… upward and upward we proceeded and with each step a new vision of this world of Yosemite greeted us… finally just before the trail sign to Babcock Lake we entered a world of ice and snow… at first it was only a few patches of snow until finally we were walking in a world still locked in the grasp of winter… slowly we plodded onward… i don't know how we missed the next trail junction, but we missed the side trail to Babcock Lake and therefore walked an extra two and a half miles to Emeric Lake… the ice blue waters of the lake, locked and still sleeping in their winter coat was worth the extra miles… from the snowfields that bordered the lake we practiced our self-arrest techniques and glissaded down the snowy slopes again and again until we both had our fill… around 2:00 p.m. we began our six mile hike back to Lake Merced…

with our downward trekking we kept a slow but steady pace… slowly my knees and feet began to feel each mile as we descended from this world of winter… suddenly a loud noise of a fast moving object alarmed us and revealed a beautiful black bear … the bear stopped and looked up at us surprisingly, wondering what we were doing in his world, only to lope off again… indeed this was a good journey today, and we now walked within the silence of our own thoughts… slowly we drifted down the remaining miles down to our camp…

a fire framed our evening again… the fire was small but provided the warmth that bonded our friendship as we talked… lifelong friends even though tomorrow we all shall part forever… i always pray i remember these friends and these moments we shared… our time was good, but each of us must walk the trails we find… i wonder how many more campfires my life will have… and to you my love, i thank you, sleep well and may our dreams be of each other…

June 7, 2014
Merced Lake

last night i enjoyed my best night's sleep… i question, was i finally settling into my mountain rhythm or was i just tired from the day's hike up to Emeric Lake… i found myself tossing and turning, but it was interspersed with peaceful sleep… i awoke around 4 a.m. and after that had a hard time falling back to sleep… i filled that empty time with memories of the blessings of nature that my boots have taken me to during the past years… finally around 7 a.m. with an early morning chill hanging heavy in the air, i rolled out of my tent…

automatically, without any thought, the morning ritual began... i aired out my sleeping bag, started my stove while trying to stay warm till my hot Tang could warm my inner core... i wandered over to where Austin was breaking down his camp to bid my farewell to him as he would head up to Sunrise... in a way i was glad we were parting our ways as once again i would have the solitude that i so greatly enjoy... after i finished my Tang and some oatmeal i headed up a steep slope of granite rock until i was at a level that marked the top of the forest's canopy... there i found my perch and sat while the early rays of a morning sun warmed my back... i sat without any real purpose other than to enjoy basking in the sun... my thoughts drifted randomly as the minutes slipped silently past... eventually i came down and finished packing up my gear for the day's hike to Washburn Lake... hiking now, with only my shadow, i was in no real rush to keep pace with another set of boots, so i found an easy pace to enjoy my solitude... the trail wandered by the Merced River, as it alternated between beautiful cascades and then into a leisurely flow as the elevation leveled out... the trail seemed to drift randomly through the forest, at times dramatic exposures would open up showing an array of endless granite gorges... many a times i stopped to record the beauty of Yosemite with my camera, but i always knew i would never really be able to capture the essence of Yosemite's soul... even though my camera has colored countless canvases over the years i always know, in the end, i really have to etch these images into my memory, for photos never capture the magic... finally i reached Washburn Lake only to be greeted with the most charming lake i've seen since the Enchanted Lakes of the Washington Cascades... framing the lake were the peaks of the Clark Range still dressed in their winter whites, while massive fortress-like walls formed two borders of the lake... along the side of this granite wall, and the shoreline of this lake, a narrow trail wandered past trees and boulders ending where i'll never know... instead of continuing onward i found a rock on the shore of the lake and sat and read while i witnessed the slow movement of the sun across the sky... i read and napped until i was eventually robbed of the warmth of the late afternoon sun… after gathering my stuff, i wandered down the trail until i found another rock to sit on and read for a while more… soon i realized i would have to begin my slow hike back down to my campsite at Merced Lake… the time passed too quickly with my boots leading me downward… upon reaching my camp, i unloaded my day pack, found my yellow collapsible bucket and headed back to Merced Lake to take a refreshing bucket bath washing away the miles… with bucket after bucket of cold water i baptized myself, awakening every muscle and fiber in my body until i truly felt cleansed and refreshed… afterwards i washed my socks and shirt and then made my way back to my campsite… the rest of my late afternoon was spent napping and reading as tomorrow i shall head down again to Little Yosemite Valley camp… after all this hiking my knees are really beginning to feel the miles and unfortunately i realize i must now amend my hiking plans… my several weeks in the backcountry will have to be cut drastically short… after all this beauty and solitude, i dread the awaiting crowded campground, filled with too many voices… i know i will enjoy my day's hike down to the valley tomorrow, as much as i did hiking up to Merced Lake several days ago… that hike greeted me with so many dramatic viewpoints, and i know they all await my eyes yet again… tonight my thoughts drift to Joanne's and my trip later this summer… i love you my love and miss you… keep me safe on my trails with your prayers…

June 8, 1991

Backpacker's Camp, Yosemite Valley

as the day was just starting to break, i broke my camp… the sky was a bright blue and scattered with high cirrus stratus clouds… with that i knew the weather would be changing in a day or possibly sooner (a reliable way to predict a future weather change is with an increase in the amount of high cirrus clouds)… after finishing putting my pack together, i began my day's hike at a good steady pace, for the miles would be many, and tried to enjoy all that was before me… within hours the sky began to get overcast and the clouds stole some of the dramatic light that colored the rocks… the hike through what i called Merced Canyon was still breath-taking, and often i had to stop to etch this canvas into my memory… the miles began to slip away as i found a good rhythm with my hike… unfortunately as i continued hiking, my natural rhythm was broken and my hike became a forced race to the valley… it always seems my homebound hikes end up this way… so with my knees beginning to ache, i decided to hike all the way down to the Backpacker's Camp in Yosemite Valley rather than stay in the Little Yosemite Campground… originally i had planned a total of two days to hike down to the valley instead of the thirteen plus miles i would put behind me today… my boots put mile after mile behind me, and i knew i was making good time… my rhythm became steady again and my shoulders carried my pack surprisingly well without really any problem…

in only 5.5 hours i had walked the 13+ miles down into Yosemite Valley… one of the reasons i hiked the distance today was because as i hiked into Little Yosemite Valley Campground, i was met with far more people than what i wanted… it was still early in the day, and feeling good, i just let my boots carry me home… i kept thinking of a nice cold soda and a good shower to wash away the miles… downward i went from Nevada Falls, but now i was being slowed by the scores of day hikers and tourists… at times as i walked by these day hikers i felt i was on display… all eyes were on me, my pack must have looked enormous to these day hikers and my clothes showed the dust from the past week of hiking… as bad as i must have looked, i knew my soul had been cleansed…

later in the evening i sat once again by my tent, but now i had the image of Half Dome hovering over me… i am at peace, for i know my tent will shelter me for the next two days before i head home…

i sit now and contemplate the transition i must go through as i enter the chaos of reality… i called Joanne to tell her i was safe and all was well… for just one more day i'll stay within this valley before my long drive home… i'm still undecided as to my plans for the morrow but having put all those miles behind me in the past week i really feel good… maybe today's hike was proof that my knees are still in fairly good shape… tomorrow i'll do some bouldering or just take in the beauty of this valley before starting my long drive home… this trip was good for my soul, and now i am ready for the next journey my boots will take me on…

A Letter to John Muir

i wish i could remember when i first spoke John Muir's name or picked up a book filled with his words, but i can't… i know though that Muir's words touched my soul and changed my life in the process, and because of that i slowly became a disciple of his teachings… slowly over the years his books filled my shelves, and i read and reread these books… the pages became gently worn from my fingers caressing the pages as i took his words deep into my heart… Muir wrote much about a special place that he held in his heart, Yosemite… because of his writings about this special place i knew i eventually would have to experience Yosemite for myself…

my first journey to Yosemite will always be remembered as it was early June and there was still snow in the high country… during the prior school year, i had planned a backpacking trip to spend several weeks hiking alone in the backcountry of Yosemite… i would spend several days first in Yosemite Valley with its sheer walls of granite that i knew would hold me in a dream-like world… then after a few weeks in the backcountry, i would once again head down to Yosemite Valley to spend a few days before i journeyed home…

after the morning of my last day of school, i loaded up my Jeep CJ7 and finally headed towards the land of granite domes… once in Yosemite, i planned to spend my first few nights in the "Climber's Campground" rather than among the tourists in the general campground… my first initial days were spent either walking amongst the climbers as they laid out their hardware preparing for a day's given climb, bouldering, or simply organizing my pack for the days ahead… the following words were taken from my journal written during and after that trip…

June 9, 1991
a letter to John Muir

i like to think it was he who led me down this path… other destinations in the park i could have taken, but no other walk would have moved me so for upon this path that i journeyed… i found a granite boulder with a bronze plaque, "Climb the mountains and get their glad tidings"… hymns of praise that Muir spoke from this very spot, from the cabin John built and lived in for several years, here at the foot of Yosemite Falls… even though John's cabin no longer stands here, i'm sure his door and porch faced the falls of Yosemite… and in my many travels, i stood at other places where he stood, along the hot and dusty trail that boldly descends a canyon… there sits a lonely shelter, he had also taken refuge from the relentless heat of the sun and talked with a friend, yet when i sat there not even his spirit could i feel… but now, as i stand and throw my head upwards to admire the heavenly waters of the Yosemite Falls, i not only feel John's presence but i know John's spirit is with me…

John, i wonder, if we now took a walk through this valley that you loved so dearly, would a tear of happiness or sorrow appear… now that the soft valley meadows of your garden have been harden by the paths of man… John, this valley that you walked and loved is slowly being torn apart and i fear for its future… they all come as we did though, to admire this creation, yet their admiration is of a different beat and slowly the valley changes… but fear not John, for a day's walk into the woods, and a good day's walk it must be, one can find your spirit with every voyager who wanders the trails…

how many times did i stop to feel the bark on a tree or take the time to count the rings of a fallen tree… to step around so as not to crush a newly formed flower… to sit upon the granite and feel the polished surface, the warmth from a hot afternoon sun… or to feel the silent coolness of the coming of the night… to stand in a silence admiring a creek, the pebbles an assortment of colors and shapes that sparkle in the cool and clear bronze waters… John you would have loved the Merced this time of year, for it ran with such a force and beauty that you could not help but be hypnotized by its power… and John i too sat by the fire at night, like you often did and became absorbed in this display of colors, for the flames were not just oranges and blues but laced with every color of the rainbow… John, i often sat upon the ground to do nothing but to feel its comfort… i would read and even write of its beauty… how many pine cones did i touch, the sap still sticky… John, Yosemite is still in the back country, and yes it's well-traveled, but the caretakers all are of your spirit… after all John, if not for you our paths may never have crossed in this garden… so as i prepare to leave with the rising sun, and though my feelings are mixed as to the pictures that were painted before me in this valley, i'll choose to remember a distant river that flowed with your wild spirit downward from the snow covered peaks, through canyons carved in granite, cascading yet flowing so proudly… i'll see the granite domes with the fading sun setting low in the summer sky… the tall pines reaching upwards to the heavens while fallen warriors are now waiting out their last years… and that special silent spot from where you stood countless times admiring the magic of Yosemite Falls… thank you John

jtalarico

Wanderings along the
Oregon Coast

with the ending of each school year, my wife and i would load up
our little Coleman camper, and with our two dogs, spend parts of
many summers driving north along the California coast following
Highway 1… we would camp wherever we felt the need, as there
was never a timeframe for any of the endless beaches along this
coast… like two gypsies we just wandered with the wind along a
highway heading north…

below are journal entries written along the coast of Oregon…

July 1991
a beach somewhere along the Oregon coast
for the past week i have been blessed to live with the sounds of the
sea… to watch the drifting of the fog as it rode silently on the winds,
slowly adding a mystical charm that one could only feel but not
touch… the rhythm of the tides became my time-keeper… the salt
air would constantly bathe my senses, awaken them with the damp
chilling breeze that often blew along the beach as i took my
countless walks… my life became one of wandering without
purpose other than just to be close to the sea… i will miss the sand
between my toes, walking like a child on the fringes of the sea,
feeling the sun on my back and the wind through my hair… often
ankle deep in the cold water i would drift into and out of the small
waves that continually dance upon the shore… to look out to the
sea and to dream like a child… to watch the clouds as they floated
peacefully over the horizon… haunting cries of the gulls would fill
the air then fading into silence leaving only the gentle breaking of
the waves to accompany me in my solitude… i became very fond of

this new friend of mine, the coast of Oregon… i've always loved the sea, but here where the mountains are gentle, and yes the forest are soft and green, i believe my feet found a new home to wander within…

today i took a quiet journey through this world of green, where the forest floor is soft and filled with such a diversity of life… i often stopped to touch the dampness of the ferns or to view the beauty of a wildflower… to touch its beauty… to smell its fragrance… taste a ripened salmon berry or arch my head upwards to gaze at the canopy above… these silent moments when time stood still for me as i etched this canvas into a memory i will carry with me in the months ahead… occasionally i was blessed with a view of the sea, its shore always dressed with its rocky coast, sea stacks slowly weathering the rhythm of the waves… how many times did i hesitate in my wanderings along that beach, touching softly those rocks that boldly stand as castles silently along the shores… with the eyes of my father i admired their unseen beauty then slowly my footprints drifted aimlessly until i stood at the throne of yet another castle with only the haunting cries of the gulls above to accompany my soul…

thoughts of Newport, Oregon

i sit upon a terrace covered with a blanket of green laced with wildflowers… to the west the summer sun is slowly journeying to its approaching horizon against a faded and pale blue sky… the music one hears is that of the ocean… the endless breaking of the waves upon the shore… like whispers, the faint cry of the gulls sends a haunting echo through the wind… the smell of the salt refreshes one's senses… it's a peaceful calm…

these past three days along this beach have done much for my spirit as they have rekindled a love that i have always felt for the sea… after many endless voyages along the shore, wandering slowly to the rhythm of the waves with my thoughts free to drift with the fading tides, i found peace and solitude… i heard myself laugh aloud as i watched my dog prance and run with the wind… chasing the gulls and being caught by the hidden surf… her spirit was free as she ran at times without purpose, yet always to return to walk by my side… and i think of the many times Joanne's soft and fragile hand was held gently by mine as we walked in a rhythm that the years have nourished… our thoughts silent, yet her touch speaking of a thousand love poems… in the distant south, out on a rocky cove, standing alone with only the sounds of the wind, the gulls and the relentless breaking of the surf, stands a lighthouse… to me its image is one of beauty, yet to many, whose eyes would have searched frantically through the thickening fog, it must of been more of a feeling of safety… knowing a safe harbor would be soon be crystalizing out of the fog, and the cold damp winds finally fading as the warmth of its harbor was won…

somewhere to the south there can be found a beach blanketed with the weathered and worn pebbles of countless waves… black in color, the pebbles were round, and with each breaking wave the pebbles rolled about, continually rearranging their presence… the percussion of the stones broke the rhythm of the surf, while always the haunted cries of the gulls blanketed this world…

during one walk, i was one of many who stopped momentarily in their wandering… all at once a mystical solitude took over the beach as a stillness came over the rolling surf… eyes were drawn to the west, as each in their own solitude and humbled by the moment, watched a setting sun dip below the horizon… the sky wasn't ablaze in colors as i have witnessed many a times in the desert… colors painted in all the reds, blues, and purples on a canvas against a lonely desert mountain… no, this was simple, yet its simplicity leant itself to a greater beauty…

during another walk i traveled upon the warm afternoon sand… its warmth comforting to the feet as you dig your toes down deep letting the sand slip between… like a child i dragged my feet slowly… time brings back all the sand castles that have been washed away by the tides of the years… to walk along the beach, the wet sand soft, as now your toes curl and dig downward… clumps of wet sand… remember in your youth when your childlike hands would sift endlessly through the warm sands… you sat along the beach and cautiously let the waves wash upon your small legs… always ready to run for the safety of the beach with the approach of a scary wave… now i still walk through the fading surf, more assured… my feet have weathered many a storms during their youth, but still like a child my eyes are drawn to the mystifying sea… a thin fog slowly is drifting inward… images of the rocks along the coast are silently being swallowed with the approaching fog… the distant horizon fades from sight as the silhouettes of a flock of gulls are seen as they dance silently by… a calmness slowly settles upon the sea as it is quietly being blanketed by the fog… even the echoes of the gulls have now been hushed… silently the fog rolls in, only the surf can be heard as its image has been stolen from my view… my canvas now fades into a gray mist… the sun shines dimly through the haze allowing only a small pathway of the sea to be seen… ghostly silhouettes of images fade only to return again… upon the sand, the remains of sand castles left randomly upon the deserted beach… the multitudes of deserted footprints await the incoming tide… a time for a cleansing… a new beginning awaits with each fading tide… and once again a child can be the first to build his sand castle to stand majestically against the recurring tide… to stand the test of time… then only to crumble again…

July 1991
suitcases of memories… wanderings
from along the beaches of Oregon

as i sit now with pen in hand and record these images, a sadness slowly builds within… it's always hard to leave the side of a good friend, for i will miss dearly the many moments that you have shared in my secrets and solitude… when i wake and slowly fade into the distant miles along this coastal highway, who will follow the fading impressions of my wandering footprints left behind… listen to your gull's cries and feel the tears of a misty fog bathing the shoreline… stand in silence as the setting sun slowly bids a lonely farewell to yet another day… and as time marches on, so will your waves continue to wash upon your shores, to slowly leave their gentle touch upon the the empty sands… and as eternal as the rhythm of the waves upon your shores are, so will be my love for thee… farewell dear friend, i bid thee well to weather the storms that you shall face, for you have touched deeply upon my spirit as i have now left a part of me here to wait by your shore through the long winter's fog for the moment when once again i can touch your soul as you have touched mine…

jtalarico

A Moment by a Mountain

July 1991

Mt. Rainier, WA

for almost a week i sought your image… and with each passing hour i had to accept that even though i knew your presence was near, your reflection would be denied until the moment was right… like a true sailor i kept my sight marked on your horizon… i weathered the hours and my faith held true… late in the day, when my thoughts were few, and my shoulders ached from my heavy pack, and my feet were tired, i happened to catch your reflection with an unintended glance… there upon the horizon, within the throne of the clouds faded against the tired blue afternoon sky you waited… i can still remember like it was yesterday… i stopped, for i was held under your spell… a smile reflected my silent inner joy… after only a few moments my boots took me away from that spot, and in the passing of empty minutes, i could not help believing i would have easily accepted my chosen lot if you had insisted and not shown your face… i learned to have patience with nature… i always recall John Muir's words, "With every walk in nature one receives far more than he seeks"… i learned that you must carry the patience of a wise wanderer and leave your expectations far behind… and what i was granted, in just those a few passing moments, would last for many days until i would return…

a year later…

i heard you whispering in my dreams and i came again… it was in the early morning hours with the clouds hanging low and a fine rain gently falling that my boots guided me once again… there were no stars to guide me, to be my compass, when what i seek cannot be found… i traveled my determined course, for this trail had become my compass… and once again my faith held strong… for even though i could not see you, i could feel your presence… a strange chill came over my tired body… i stopped, knowing not why but knowing i had to… and then the skies silently began to slowly open and their colors gave hope to our rendezvous… my footsteps instinctively hurried as i traveled through this forest, for i did not want these guardians of your world to hide you from my sight… i began to feel the silent peace that blanketed your feet in this old growth forest that carpets and surrounds you… time and time again i thrust my head upward and followed the noble lines of the cedars that stood guard along this path, and with each clearing in the forest, my eyes searched frantically for your reflection… as the miles drifted by so did the clouds against the promising blue sky… once again when my thoughts were drifting, with the solitude of the passing forest, i happened to steal upon your image… and even though that moment passed too quickly, my spirit cried aloud in joy… now the miles seemed to pass by even more slowly, as that moment within your reflection was not enough to satisfy my thirst for your presence… my footsteps were not many until against a pure blue canvas i saw your full reflection… it was painted with the most majestic colors and all i could do was to stop in silence and in prayer… a silent reverence overcame those minutes that passed by… motionless i stood as if my movements would cause this picture to fade away… and now as the day slowly passed i was blessed with your image time and time again against the late afternoon sky… at times the clouds would hang low and hide your summit from my view… with the eyes of my father i witnessed the subtle changes as the sun slowly followed its course against that tired afternoon sky… at times my eyes would try to focus on every little detail of your face, etching those lines deep within my memory… other times it was not your full reflection that i would paint, and in those moments i learned to appreciate the gift of your full reflection…

it was upon your lower slopes, late in the afternoon, that my restless spirit had to silently witness the reflection of voyagers as they struggled silently to grace upon your lonely summit... i wished that it was me upon your mighty slopes, but all i could do was stand witness and envy the reflection of those who climbed upward... i knew they would be tired from the relentless heat of the sun and the endless procession of steps that they had to endure... i remembered when i too was dressed with a heavy pack and coils of rope, an ice ax as my staff, with my black and worn crampons strapped to my boots... mountain paint would protect their sunburnt faces as it did mine... and then after all the hardship they endured there would be those priceless moments... that certain look... yes, i too can remember my smile that told of those precious few moments upon a summit... my pain was alive with jealousy as i watched their silent parade... promises raced through my heart as i would time and time again rest my eyes towards your summit... my restless footsteps will have to wade through many a storms for that hopeful time... later in the day, as it was quietly ending, i stood amongst those that dream not as i... a crowd of travelers stood with reverence... we had to stand and silently witness as the night silently erased your image... i call you my white goddess and your reflection will silently grace my winter dreams until the winter snows melt and the days grow longer... then i promise, i too will wear the coils of rope and begin the slow dance that shall take me, if i may be blessed, upon your summit...

jtalarico

Flying Home from Mt. Rainier

thoughts as i fly over the Canyonlands of Arizona

the land below me now appears brown and barren but i know better, for i have walked many times within the Canyonlands that make up this part of Arizona… once again i am in Arizona, and no longer do i see the carpet of green that formed the forest of the places i've left… even from these heights, as i look down upon my canyon, i can touch it all from my memory… the insane comfort of a hot day… the silence of its vastness… the magic of this land created in a solitude from a river that now flows gently by… i have left my mountain only to return to my canyon, and with this i find out really how rich i am… i will miss my Tahoma (Mt. Rainier) but i know she will wait during the seemingly endless passage until we meet again… but for now i will find comfort in the solitude of the desert… may i find my path in the warmth of the sun as i pass the silent forest of rocks whose colors parade softly and silently by… where my sunsets are painted with every shade of red and purple… once again where my views are endless…
i am home… where the spirit of my father lives… i am home again to my desert and to you, whom i love

jtalarico
August 8, 1991

Islas De Todos Santos, Baja Norte, Mexico
October 21, 1995

the cry of the gulls fills the sky as they float amidst this greenish colored sea… the smell of salt is heavy in the air as i can almost feel it raining down upon my sun tanned skin… waves breaking freely onto a shell and pebble covered beach… a symphony of sounds from the rhythm of the breaking waves swiftly washing across the wave worn pebbles and shells… again and again, waves washing over this world… i walk the shoreline… there is no sand on this beach to leave the footprints of the moments that i spend here… once again i am in communion with the sea… my horizons, an endless sea fading into the late afternoon sun… to the east the faint blue profiles of ancient mountains on the mainland … but for the moment my home is this island… an island that i unselfishly share with countless birds, for i am in a sanctuary belonging to the gulls and pelicans… i must be careful where i walk… nesting sites, for many of these birds carpet this refuge… i wonder if the cries of these gulls are simply their love songs… thoughts of my mother who loves to hear their cries fill her world by the sea… my mother has a gift of seeing beauty in everything she witnesses… she loves these birds and their songs while others only hear the reckless noise of scavengers…

a multitude of brown pelicans hover over the sea while others stand watch on the cliffs… the air echoes endlessly with their haunting cries… i let my eyes drift towards the sea, the swells are broken by the antics of sea lions playing in the green waters… the wind, damp from its dance across the waters feels good on my face… in this moment i feel so alive and a part of this world that i love…

this morning as the day awakened, our kayaks quickly and orderly slid through a small surf as we left the rocky coast of Punta Banda, a peninsula jutting out into Todos Santos Bay about 30 miles south of Ensenada, Mexico... leaving the safety of the shore behind us we began our paddling across the open waters to this island... our kayaks strung out randomly... a parade of colorful images that dotted this endless sea of green as we slowly made our way... i sat in my kayak, so close to the water that i felt i was one with the sea... my kayak an extension of my essence...i became the sea and the sea became me... the endless rhythm of the swells slowly pushed us onward... at times i would be alone within these swells, my companions all hidden by these watery giants... a sea lion poked its head into the cool air to see who was intruding into his world, then was gone in a moment, no trace left behind of those moments we shared...

i am in love with the endless rhythm of the swells upon this sea... my world was now simply the sea... in that moment of time i never wanted to let these minutes end... my thoughts drifted randomly throughout this voyage... my arms paddled in an endless repetition of motion, without thought but with purpose... the endless march of the swells towards some distant shore... even with the giant swells, the sea that i paddled across was gentle, but i could sense its strength... a gentle breeze stirred the air, yet in a moment it can change showing its angry face... to be at the mercy of this sea... thoughts that lingered as i watched the gentleness of the swells... promises were made again and again... i will, no i must, return to this world that my kayak has led me to...

Later in the day as evening approaches i sit upon a rock overlooking a steep cliff that forms one side of this island... the rock looking out towards the sea... just hours ago i journeyed across that sea... dusk is still hours away, another Mexican sunset awaits... my thoughts return to the sea i left... magic moments that ended all too quickly... i sing a silent prayer to the sea in thanks...

October 22, 1995
Sitting in a motel in San Diego

the cries of the gulls no longer fill my world… as i sit in an unwanted silence i feel the emptiness of what i left behind… the air is stale within the confines of my motel room… i struggle with the fact that i had to leave… my time there was too short… all i have to comfort me in these moments are the memories i stole… i question if these fragments of moments will be enough for my soul in the coming days…

i slept last night listening to the steady pulse of the surf upon the beach… the air was filled with a haunting silence without the cries of the gulls… a gray mist settled over the island only to be shattered by the light from a lonely lighthouse… a beacon of warning to those who work upon this sea…

morning broke… the sea was calm with only the gentle swells from distant shores… i lingered in those moments trying to hold on to their essence… a mug of Tang warmed my hands… slowly i tore down my tent and formed the piles of gear that i would place in my kayak… this ritual was new to me… no longer would my backpack hold my world… with our kayaks loaded we sat on this beach with our thoughts, alone yet amongst each other… the sea was calling… one by one our kayaks slid across the pebbled beach into the awaiting sea… our dance across this bay waited until the shore let go of the last of our kayaks… then slowly we began our slow parade towards home

but first we would circumnavigate the island… once again the air filled with the cries of the gulls bidding us a safe journey homeward… we paddled far off the northern portion of the island as it was washed by a deadly surf… not only could i see the strength of this sea by the crashing of these huge waves upon the cliffs, but also i could feel it pulling me… drawing me into a surf i wanted no part of…my grip tighten on my paddle… with strong strokes, one after another, i kept my distance… through a small strait separating the islands we paddled... i could feel the sea coming alive as we paddled along this last stretch of coastline until it was time to bid farewell and begin our crossing...

my world now became the constant swells pushing us homeward... i felt alive, full of life... we paddled onward, at times each of us lost in our solitary thoughts... other times our laughter and chatter would break the silence... at times i was able to find and catch the rhythm of the swells...my kayak surfing freely onward... at times lost in thought, i dreamed of places i now wanted to see... a new sense of freedom excited me as i knew this wilderness of ocean i paddled within is endless... sea lions playing within the surf, the roar of their barks joined now with the cries of the gulls... we paddled into the cove of La Bufadora... a forest of kelp filled the sea... i began to prepare for my landing, wondering if there would be a surf or just the gentle pulses of the tides... all too soon i felt the sand of the beach as it scraped my kayak... just like that i realized my journey was over...

the rhythm of the highway replaced that of the sea as we moved across a sea of concrete... once again, homeward bound

jtalarico

Kayaking Mulege to Loreto

This was one of many trips I took with Southwest Kayak, led by the famed long-distance kayaker Ed Gillette. Ed became known to the kayaking world after his solo paddle from Monterey California, to Hawaii in 1987.

The trip that I was about to undertake was to be an eight-day, 75-mile exploration in the Sea of Cortez, along the coast between Mulege and Loreto, Baja Mexico. We would car caravan from Southwest Kayak's store in San Diego down to Mulege, Mexico. This would be my first multi-day, long distance kayak trip in coastal waters, so I was a little hesitant, as I really didn't know what to expect, and if my newly acquired kayaking skills were up to this trip.

Excerpt from John Steinbeck's
The Log from the Sea of Cortez

"Trying to remember the Gulf is like trying to re-create a dream. This is by no means a sentimental thing, it has little to do with beauty or even conscious liking. But the Gulf does draw one, and we have talked to rich men who own boats, who can go where they will. Regularly they find themselves sucked into the Gulf. And since we have returned, there is always in the backs of our minds the positive drive to go back again. If it were lush and rich, one could understand the pull, but it is fierce and hostile and sullen. The stone mountains pile up to the sky and there is little fresh water. But we know we must go back if we live, and we don't know why."

John Steinbeck

December 29, 1995
Mulege, Mexico
(notes written after a two day drive south)

we drove deep into a name that lately i spoke of often, Baja, Mexico,

161

and even though i was hundreds of miles into this land i still did not know what to expect… it seemed we drove endlessly south throughout those two days… i sat silently gazing out the window… the desert drifted by while i was held prisoner in this car… i wanted so badly to reach out and touch what i was falling in love with, but i couldn't… i had walked the Arizona desert and studied its geology for years, but why do i feel this desert is so different… is the desert of Baja, Mexico, really any different than what i've seen before in Arizona… i kept asking myself this question as the sun painted its arc across the sky… i was still in the Sonoran Desert that i fell in love with so many years ago, but now i was in the Vizcaino sub division (according to biologists) of this desert, heading south towards the Sea of Cortez…

after we left the small coastal town of El Rosario behind, with the freedom of the gulls floating in their sea of salt air, we started to head into the the high dry desert of Central Baja… the faded mountains of the Sierra San Miguel Mountains were a constant refection towards the north as the vegetation became one that i had grown accustomed to in the deserts of Arizona, cactus amongst an ocean of weathered granite… mile after mile i looked out at this desert… Steinbeck's Sea of Cortez seemed a lifetime away as the miles turned into hours… finally as the sun began its slow path to the west, lunch was taken in Catavina where i saw my first boojum tree, a mystical tree from the likes of Alice in Wonderland… hidden secrets this land had begun to reveal to me… the chatter around our lunch table was alive with excitement as we all listened to Ed, like children sitting in a classroom, we were enchanted by his tales of this desert and the sea that we would hopefully see soon…

with our lunch behind us, the endless drone of our tires on this weary highway continued… the darken blue silhouettes of the Sierra San Miguel Mountains were replaced by those of the volcanic mountains of the Sierra La Asamblea range to our distant east… staring at these mountains, we found it was hard to believe that our destination, the Sea of Cortez was within a hour's drive away from those mountains…

with the cool air and the darken skies of night upon us, we stopped for the night in the town of Guerrero Negro, the Gateway to the Laguna Ojo de Liebre or its better known name, Scammon's Lagoon, the birthing and mating waters of the Gray Whales… this town sits along the 28th parallel line that divides California (Norte), which we had officially left, and Baja California Sur… a 140' tall steel eagle monument marks this location… it was in this town that we would have to go through another immigration checkpoint which would officially let us enter Baja California Sur…

after a quick dinner we scattered our tarps across the desert ground of a makeshift campground to await our last day's drive towards our destination of Mulege…

late in the afternoon, of our second day of driving south, and after leaving the town of San Ignacio behind us, we started to make our way to the eastern coast of Baja and the Sea of Cortez… it wasn't until we ended a tortuous drive of twisting, turning switchbacks that the highway finally leveled out and we saw our first view of the sea that soon we would journey upon… that first reflection of this endless expanse of water brought excitement to us all but i sat in isolated silence thinking…

my mind raced back and forth as i remembered that i had been on many bodies of waters in my lifetime yet why did i feel this would be unlike anything i had seen before… i had been reading the words of Steinbeck's *Log from the Sea of Cortez*… the pages are filled with my scribbled notes, thoughts and impressions, yet i'm still not sure what awaits…

i asked myself, why was i taking this journey… why now…

i recently reread parts of Thoreau's *Walden* as i continually attempt to bring simplicity back into my life… i question in this world today, is this even possible… i journey on this quest hoping to feel the spirit of this restless sea, yet i swim in a sea of modern conveniences… a Gore Wear sleeping bag bought because i'm always hiking in a wet area and i want to stay warm in a dry bag… polypropylene everything… my jacket is also Gore Wear… an inflatable air mattress that i've used to help keep me comfortable on a hard ground… i laugh now at all the simplicity that i have accumulated to enhance my enjoyment… did any of this really give me a greater sense of experiencing the wilderness… what price have i paid in achieving my version of a simpler existence…

i was taking this journey also to be one with the sea again… memories of my childhood summers in the salt air amongst the endless cries of the gulls helped form this bond with the ocean… and of this Sea of Cortez, maybe i just want to feel and enjoy its many faces that Steinbeck wrote about in his book…

as the day slipped into dusk, we pulled into a campground beside the Mulege River which flows into the Sea of Cortez… tired yet excited we laid out our tarps and unloaded our gear to be sorted in the morning… darkness and a scattering of trees and buildings hid the sea from us all, but that would soon change…
in the morning i shall load my kayak and begin my journey, a journey to listen to the sea and follow wherever it shall take me…

December 28, 1995
written on a beach south of Punta Concepcion
reflecting on my first day on the water

we awoke… it still seemed like it was in the middle of the night… the stars were bright as they filled this early morning sky… dawn was still a few hours away… slowly, as i have done so many times in the past, i began the gradual task of packing… i chose last night to sleep under the stars, so my sleeping bag was damp from the dew that fell upon us like rain… instead of packing my backpack, as i have done for ages now, i had the new task of loading my kayak… this ritual was new and strange to me… my movements were awkward, as i had to continually stop and think where something should go... slowly my two waterproof hatches, in my sea-faring kayak, got filled but still items were spread out before me... whereas i would always strap gear on the outside of my pack, now i started to secure seabags to both the forward and rear decks of my kayak... as i finished this task i felt an excitement starting to fill my soul despite feelings of apprehension as to what i would encounter as the day unfolded... i am journeying within an ocean that i am still trying to feel comfortable and confident in...

eventually the fading night was filled with sounds of kayaks being dragged from the beach into the awaiting water... finally it was my turn... without time to grasp this moment, i was taken from the security of the beach into the Mulege River... quickly i got myself oriented and secured my spray skirt as i drifted away from the shore... once all the kayaks were launched we let the river's current take us out to sea... my journey in this sea was now beginning... the stars were still shining brightly overhead as my paddle began a movement that i would repeat countless times throughout the day... up ahead i could make out the darken silhouettes of other kayakers... conversation broke the stillness of this night as we now began our silent parade out to Bahia de Santa Ines... often the stillness would be broken by our voices, but our voices were soft and gentle as if we were afraid to break this sacred silence of the fading night... towards the east the sky began to lighten and the stars faded as dawn approached... what took place in the next moments was like a miracle as the sky became alive with a golden and rose red glow that reflected far out into the bay... we left the gentleness of the river and now paddled out into the swells of the awaiting bay... as dawn broke over the sea, one had to believe that this creation was a gift from the gods being bestowed on us... my senses were flooded with this magic unfolding before me... i felt an unexplainable spiritual high and therefore offered my prayers in thanks... thoughts of my father and a mountain guide that took me to a lonely mountain summit many summers in my past... i thought of my wife, my best friend, and thanked her time and time again in my prayers… time stood still in these moments…

slowly my body picked up the rhythm of the sea… swell after swell that now would carry me throughout this journey… a parade of colorful kayaks, broken and spread out across this sea, paddled onward… my paddle felt good in my hands guiding my kayak along… my kayak became just an extension of my spirit… the sea was now all around me, swallowing me up yet calling me onward… talk was small throughout the day as we all let this sea spread our parade apart… off to my right was the silhouette of the land slowly passing… a land harsh and unforgiving yet filled with familiar images… shades of brown that painted the distant mountains… the smell of the sea was heavy in the air and i could taste the salt of the sea on my face… hours passed… stroke after stroke of my paddle, a never-ending repetition until there was sand under my kayak as it was being dragged onto the beach… the day at sea had ended

December 29, 1995

Punta Santa Teresa

(an unexpected ditch camp to avoid the rough afternoon sea) our camp last night, south of Punta Concepcion, was on a small rocky beach nestled close to the high tide mark… ghostly sounds of a rising tide were heard throughout the night… i was tired from my first long hard day of kayaking and slept soundly, but it seemed morning came in the middle of the night as we woke only to find the stars carpeting a clear sky… i fired up my little stove and soon had my mug filled with hot Tang along with a bowl of oatmeal… the breakfast of champions, at least that's what i believe… slowly our camp was broken down as small piles of gear laid scattered on the beach waiting to be stored in our kayaks… under the solitude of the stars and the first hint of a new day dawning we loaded our kayaks… today storing my gear in the hatches of my kayak seemed so much easier as i just followed what i has done the day before… the air was filled with our morning chatter as we talked about what this day would bring… soon we all were standing by our kayaks awaiting the word to start… one by one kayaks were dragged into a small surf and soon the beach laid silent and empty… a silence fell over us… all eyes were drawn towards the east to greet a rising sun… soft shades of red and pink against a pale blue sky colored the eastern horizon… we waited in silence for the sun to show its morning face from behind the coastal mountains… my thoughts drifted back to the sunset last night… the sky was a softer blue against a silver coated sea… the mountains glowed a reddish gold as the sun slipped below the mountains bidding this paradise a farewell…

as the morning passed i felt more and more the changing moods in the sea… our gentle sea was being filled with swells that were growing taller and taller… i began to feel very small and fragile in this sea that was becoming alive with its wild and restless spirit… in response i gripped my paddle tighter and tighter fighting off fears that this sea would overcome me… my eastern horizon was now broken by a sea of white caps… one could not deny the strength of this sea as it began to show its spirit… the wind was now blowing steadily from the north as we made our way southward… the Mexicans refer to this wind as el Norte, and once it began blowing it was known to be a strong and steady wind… the swells were now beginning to wash over my kayak making it harder and harder for me to make a straight track southbound… our caravan of kayaks began to get spread out, and i would often lose sight of my companions behind these mountains of swells… i was now alone on this sea when only moments ago my eyes were fixed on the kayak in front of me… i paddled on, my senses alive as i continually worked to counter balance the wind and swells… the rhythm of these swells became broken making it harder and harder to anticipate the oncoming swells… i gripped my paddle tighter and tighter determine to stay upright in my kayak… minutes turned into hours and slowly my confidence was growing and i felt a little more at ease, yet at any time i knew conditions could change drastically… behind us the northern sky was turning a nasty gray color and rapidly overtaking the faint blue skies to our south… the sea continued to wash over my kayak… i was now getting wet and cold… word was being spread to try to stay closer together and behind Ed, our leader, as he was searching for a beach and surf we could safely land in… on a small rocky beach, we ditched the growing seas to find a safe shelter for the night… it felt good to know that even in less-than-ideal sea conditions i was beginning to develop the skills needed to be a contributing member of our band of kayakers… we all started this trip at different skills levels… there were a select few that had all the skills necessary to do this trip solo… then there were several of us for whom this trip was our first real long distance trip on the open sea… i was one of those, and today once again i was proud of what i accomplished… there was a great sense of relief as i felt the rocky beach of Punta Santa Teresa under my kayak… this ended my first real look at the sea and its many faces…

on this small rocky beach there was no room for all of us to pitch our tents so we laid out our tarps the best we could… tonight stars or a cloudy sky with a possibility of rain would be our fate, we knew not…

December 30, 1995

Bahia San Basilia

(reflecting back to the morning)

morning came early again and greeted us with a star filled sky… soon silent shadows were moving about in the cool damp air of this predawn… voices were heard softly at first as one starts each day in their own solitude of thoughts… shadows moved about in this darkness and soon soft sounds become the voices of comrades in this band of voyagers… stoves were lit and fresh water was hauled from our reserves stored in our kayaks (Ed told us to secure our water jugs nightly in our kayak hatches as the gulls would peck their way into our jugs to steal our fresh water, one of the main necessities of life on this barren coast)… it would still be another day before we had access to fresh water, so we all had to be cafeful to wisely use the fresh water we had…

it seemed so strange rationing water when we were spending each day in a world of water… fresh water had become something i just took naturally for granted without any thought… even in my many hikes through the canyon or in the mountains, i always had a source of fresh water close by to rely on… so quickly had this all changed…

i was trying to use about a gallon of fresh water a day and now i had a little less a gallon left for my day's use… in the solitude of my thoughts for the coming day, i sat and enjoyed the warmth of my Tang and oatmeal while looking out at the awaiting sea… gradually our morning chatter filled the darkened silence as the ritual of packing up once again occupied all of us… i have come to treasure this ritual of starting each day before the first hint of dawn… i now realize why Ed, our leader, insists we get an early start each day as we never know when the north wind will start to blow again and there is always a given distance we must make each day to get to Loreto on time…

looking towards the eastern horizon we sensed that in moments another sunrise would take place… everything seemed to stop in anticipation of this moment… we all quietly waited… we waited in hopes of witnessing a green flash, which is an atmospheric phenomena that occurs just seconds before the sun peaks above the horizon… at that moment a flash of green light will be seen but only if the atmospheric conditions are ideal… (a green flash occurs when two optical phenomena combine: "a mirage and the dispersion of sunlight". As the sun dips below or above the horizon, the light is being dispersed through the earth's atmosphere like a prism allowing the green frequency of light to appear. www.aaas.org).

i waited in anticipation as i hoped to witness my first green flash, but as a chorus of voices screamed out in celebration i realized i had missed my opportunity…

as the sky now faded from the dark blues of predawn to the

soft red of dawn and eventually into a pale blue sky it signaled to all that at least we would have good weather in the morning… kayaks waited by the rising tide as we all finished our last minute details before we shoved off for another day… today's paddle would be a long paddle since we stopped early yesterday because of the rough seas… i wrestled with my thoughts of a long paddle and the possibility of rough seas as the day progressed… our small band of kayaks silently paddled off the beach and waited for our group to form up… a distant island painted our horizon… its faint profile haunted us throughout the day as we would camp somewhere beyond that island… the day began with calm seas under a clear blue sky which enabled us to cover a good distance in the morning.,. the rhythm of my paddling… movements that occurred without any thought… steady and strong my paddle cut into the sea as each stroke brightened my outlook as the day continued… minutes faded into hours, morning into afternoon… i blocked out all thoughts of being tired… i found that i was able to feel the rhythm of the swells and use their energy to help push me on throughout the day,.. as the seas gradually built throughout the day, i enjoyed the occasional swell that washed over my kayak… the cold water refreshed my spirit yet always reminded me of the power of this sea… the island that painted our horizon all morning soon became a mountain of rock and filled my horizon… our kayaks looked so fragile as we paddled past this fortress of volcanic rock.. along its rocky shoreline we heard the barks of the sea lions either crying out a welcome or pleading for us to leave them in peace… within minutes our sea came alive as several pods of dolphins danced within our parade… i was spellbound by this magic as it happened right before my eyes… dolphins seemed to be everywhere and then just like that the sea was empty and silent… eventually we paddled into Bahia San Basilio… pillars of rock painted white with the dropping of birds left throughout the years stood boldly welcoming us into this cove… osprey could be seen as they sat on these pillars and once again we heard the familiar cry of gulls .. pelicans now seemed to be everywhere as we slowly paddled the blue green waters of this cove… just below the blue-green waters were a scattering of reefs that we skirted as we approached our landing site… the echoes of our paddling seemed to fill the air within these minutes… the tiredness from a long day's paddle seeped from my body as i was filled with the magic of this bay…

once our kayaks were secured for the day and our tents pitched we all sorted through our grub bags and soon filled our stomachs as we planned the remainder of our afternoon… i spent time snorkeling around the many reefs amazed at what i thought was an abundance of marine life… Ed told us later that he was so sadden by the lack of marine life and how things had changed from the past, reflecting the words that Steinbeck was crying out in his log… Ed though did go out and spearfish us our dinner for the night… nothing like fresh fish tacos on an amazing beach…

hours later i sat alone by my tent with only my thoughts as i wrote the above entry into my journal…

December 31, 1995
Punta Mangles

star filled mornings have become a daily occurrence throughout this journey and because of this i've become very fond of my sunrise on the water… there's a quote that i have always loved from Richard Henry Dana's, *Two Years Before the Mast*, "Nothing will compare with the early breaking of day upon the wide ocean"… because of our morning ritual of starting our day with a sunrise over the water this quote has taken on a deeper meaning for me…

packing our kayaks today seemed so different… my deck hatches appeared empty from all the food i've eaten and my water reserves are almost gone… also hanging on all of our minds was the paddle we were facing today… Ed told us last night that today would not only be our toughest day but also our longest with a solid 20-mile plus paddle if we wanted to spend two days on Isla Coronado… i was excited in a way for this challenge as this would be a good test of my endurance kayaking… hiking trails on foot i was always confident and knew exactly what i could do and there were numerous times i put in 20-mile plus days carrying my pack... but this was different... very seldom does a trail ever change conditions during a day other than the elevation gains, but the ocean is an entirely different animal, and its mood and fury can change in minutes...

my reflection is now one with a soiled layer of salt encrusted clothes... zinc oxide, a natural part of my face, always protecting me from the desert sun... is this the reflection of a voyager paddling the Sea of Cortez... sand has now become a common condiment that is found everywhere within my gear and even food... as we have each previous day, we launched our kayaks into the predawn sea and began our slow paddle out of this beautiful cove... i'm falling in love with kayaking as i feel such a communion with the sea that i love... it feels so good being on the sea again, especially as we paddle towards the rising sun... our early morning is blessed with a light wind as we paddle south... once again throughout the day the sea came alive with dolphins, as they swam within an arm's reach of me, they danced and slid swiftly yet so effortlessly through the blue green waters... their freedom was felt... their beauty unmatched... in a quiet envy i watched their ballet across and through this sea...

we stopped for a lunch break on a beach and rested while the gulls filled the sky screaming for our food... always the sea awaits... the rhythm of the swells never ceasing... our lunch break ended quickly as we realized that El Norte, the North Wind had arrived... we paddled out again to a sea filled with white caps and still a ten mile stretch to paddle... the sea was now crossing my bow off my right side as the waves washed over me again and again... i realized that i would have to adjust my paddling to counteract the wind and sea... my spirit was alive and it felt so good... instead of fear i felt my confidence and welcomed this challenging sea as it baptized me time and time again... with the increase in the wind there was now an air of caution amongst this parade... we each fought our silent battles through this sea slowly pushing our way... a change in plans now had Punta Mangles as our designated ditch camp to get out of the increasing wind… just around the point in the shelter from the wind we paddled into a small cove with a sense of urgency… finally along a small rocky shore we landed our kayaks feeling safe but in a way missing that pulse of energy that filled our souls from the sea… (we made our ditch camp today because if we were to proceed to our designated beach it would have involved paddling with a strong crosswind off to our side which would have increased our chance of flipping over in the water… water rescue in strong winds and seas can be more dangerous, so Ed decided on the side of safety and ditched us early along the coast that we always followed and hugged)…

tonight instead of a sky filled with fireworks, i had my star-filled heavens and the sound of a gentle surf to welcome in a new year… instead of champagne, it was just fresh water that tasted just as good, if not better… i retreated early from the others for the solitude of my tent to reflect on the year that just slipped by… it was a blessed year

January 1, 1996
after our short-day paddle to Isla Coronado

we slept in a little later today as our paddle today would be a short passage to Isla Coronado… even though i was able to sleep in a little later, i missed waking to the solitude of my star-filled sky… instead my tent, already awaken by the early colors of the sun, reminded me that i had stayed within the warmth of my sleeping bag much too long for a traveler upon this sea… by force of habit i automatically lit my stove to heat up water for my oatmeal and Tang… i believe i will never get tired of my traditional breakfast of oatmeal and Tang… it doesn't matter where my boots, and now my paddle, take me, oatmeal and Tang will always start my day…

we quickly moved through our morning ritual of breaking camp and packing our kayaks in order to enjoy almost a whole day of relaxing on a beautiful island… the sound of the sand and pebbles sliding under our kayaks came quickly as Isla Coronado, still distant yet fully in sight, encouraged us that this would be an easy morning paddle (Isla Coronado is an island protected by the Mexican government, and since it is only a short paddle from Loreto, it is often visited by many locals for a day in the sun or a short weekend retreat).

Our paddles slid through the water cleanly and swiftly as the island came into full view… drifting white sand dunes and an endless beach scattered with palms painted this canvas before us… it seemed in no time at all the sand was under our kayaks as they were being pulled upon the beach… quickly we all were running about looking for a place to make our own… there were several palapas (an open-sided dwelling with a thatched roof made of dried palm leaves that are very common on Mexican beaches) scattered along this section of beach, and i was lucky to find one to make my own for the night …

there would be no need to pitch my tent tonight, so i simply laid out my tarp with my dry bags taken from my kayak… i left my food and water secured in my kayak, away from the curious and probably hungry gulls that were welcoming us to their island… soon the warmth of an early afternoon sun was felt on my shoulders as i took a solitary walk along the water's edge… a kaleidoscope of thoughts, my days upon this sea and lonely walks along countless beaches during my life, accompanied me as i wandered with no destination, just an endless beach with the tide and sand washing over my feet…

i had always enjoyed the bonding of travelers, thrown together on their journeys, stories told and laughter shared, but i am a solitary person and treasure my moments alone… this afternoon i gave myself the gift of just being alone with only my thoughts… how long i walked that beach, i don't know, but the time eventually came when i missed the laughter of my new found friends and discovered them gathered in a circle, sharing a bottle of spirits from the blue agave plant (tequila)… other bottles soon appeared and a tarp was laid out with all the food we did not consume throughout our trip... we toasted to our friendship and to this sea that we all had shared because we knew that within two days our paths would take us all away from these days we shared upon this sea...

time stood still throughout the rest of this day, but evening still came... alone once again, and now looking at a sky filled with stars, i used my headlamp to shine upon my journal as i recorded my thoughts from this day...

January 2, 1996
Driving back to San Diego
(we had spent the night on Isla Coronado)

once again, and for the last time, we rose with the stars to get an early start on a long day... stoves were lit and water boiled as we packed up our kayaks for our last paddle of the trip... chatter filled the silence as we reminisced about the days that had slipped by only too quickly, and to the two day drive back to our previous lives... once our paddles began to break the stillness of the early morning sea, it seemed like it was no time until the sand of the beach was under our kayaks for the last time...

another trip had ended... gear wet, weary, and waiting to be sorted and then stored was thrown on our last beach... slowly my kayak relinquished the last of my gear... a tired mess that served me well... sadly my days would no longer be filled with the blue green sea that was left behind me now... no longer would it set the course of my day... the north wind could blow hard over this sea as i would no longer be at its mercy... a certain amount of control had returned to my life, but with this gain i now lost a new and beloved friend... thoughts would always remain of this parting as it seemed i always leave a part of me behind on all my journeys... my memory would have to hold on to all the laughter and the quiet moments when the rhythm of the tides was all i wanted to hear.. as i waited to take my seat in the van, i looked out upon this sea for maybe my last time... a friend stood silently by my side... did he too feel a part of him being torn away... would our tomorrows be better than our yesterdays… a tearing between memories and dreams… both are so hard to hold on to at times like this, endings and beginnings…

this sea will never be the same to me as it once was, just a name… now this name will stir feelings and memories that have changed a small part of me… with every journey one changes ever so much, and you can never return to where you originally were…

an hour north of our last beach we stopped for a meal… we celebrated and feasted in this little oasis overlooking the sea that we all fell in love with…sadden to leave yet anxious to continue, we raised our glasses for one last toast to a sea that stole our hearts…

once again i sat looking out the car window, but now as one with a little better understanding of this desert and sea that Steinbeck spoke of in his Log… the miles and hours slowly passed as i revisited sections of a book that had journeyed with me… i was tired and ready to feel the comfort of clean white sheets against my tan body… beginning our long drive homeward there was a heavy silence that hung in the air against the endless hum of the tires on this highway heading north… like me, were the others absorbed in their thoughts of moments we brought back from our time with the gulls and the sea… the worn pages of my book took on new notes now from one who had experienced just a small part of this sea…

Several days later at home my gear has been cleaned and stored away for yet unplanned future trips… the lather of soap in a hot shower, and a clean shirt, free of the salt-encrusted world that i left, feels so good… it always feels good to be home, but there is always an emptiness in my heart for what i left behind… a book i carried with me for days, its pages worn, tired and, scribbled on has found its place among the other books in my library… my life continues on, but i know that soon new books will find their way into my hands, always leading me to a better understanding of who i am and another journey…

A Walk along the Jersey Shore

During a Christmas break from my job teaching high school biology.

i was visiting my mother… she had a small Cape Cod style house in Ship Bottom, New Jersey, located a block off the ocean… during my visit i would wake up early every day to walk the beach… it was in the early hours of the mornings, with only my shadow and the sounds of the gulls to keep me company… i forget what jacket i wore, but i know i had my black woolen Greek fishing cap on to keep my head warm and most likely a red woolen scarf that i wore a lot during those years… my boots… just another pair of hiking boots that walked with me during those years…

when i returned from my walk i got a warm fire burning in the fireplace to enjoy with a mug of hot tea and one of many beautiful talks i shared with my mother (during that visit)…

some of life's journeys are short but will last a lifetime…

December 28, 1993

it's a gray and cloudy day with a misty rain quietly falling with the shadows of summer lying hidden beneath the stillness of this winter… on a lonely beach, with only the gulls to listen to my footsteps, i drift slowly along… my footsteps now gently erase the multitude of prints that were carelessly and without thought left by the gulls… the wind is gentle yet filled with the salty smell of a winter ocean… and on this canvas, painted in lonely shades of gray, the ocean plays its haunting symphony to my ears, and with each breaking of the waves i wander back farther into my youth… many lost summers ago, in my childhood, my small feet walked this beach… and though the years silently passed by, the one constant on this beach has always been the haunting rhythm of the sea… the flooding and the ebbing of the tides that marked out their dance throughout the day… day after day and season after season this rhythm played on… but my thoughts, how different they must have been as that child… why do i now yearn for those lost summer days… what am i searching for that i felt i lost in my youth other than the innocence of my childhood… i walked this beach then without the wisdom of the years, years that have taught me to stop and listen to the music of this gray and desolate ocean… now i've learned to touch the mystical soul of this sea and listen more clearly to its songs… songs that play endlessly amongst the damp and chilly winds… (and) always the haunting cries of the gulls fill the air around me… are they the butterflies within this meadow and if so, where are the flowers that would fill the air with their silent fragrance… instead, a different fragrance paints my senses… the bitter sting of the salt air from a cold and abandoned winter wind etches deep into my soul… the wind blows silently ashore, only to creep across this empty beach, unseen and felt only by the gulls… the laughter of endless summer days are now lost on this beach as only the grays of winter must pass by slowly amid the silence left by the naked trees of this season… i wonder as one walks, can they see the beauty on this canvas or does one anxiously sweep this aside and think only of the days of summer… for this wandering voyager, i ask only for the solitude of this gray and cloudy day, the endless rhythm of the sea playing a symphony for the gulls and these damp winds which chill me… i wander today without purpose, and it's good to know that only the sea will erase my time along this shore but not my memory of this walk…

jtalarico

Philadelphia Folk Festival
August 2001

The faint whispers of bagpipes like a gentle approaching fog have been blown away now by the fading moments of time... and now too, those simple wooden stages are quiet and with them the rainbow fields of color have vanished... silent empty echoes are now all that can be heard...and your tired body is all that remains...this airport in which i wait for my life's walk to continue is quiet, yet as i sit here among the silent shadows, i can not avoid the parade of feelings that flood my tired mind, and with these feelings comes a pain... these moments are gone... and now another separation... another good-bye... when will we laugh again...

i still remember... like children standing in a Christmas line... we waited anxiously for the moments when we would rush forward through the entrance gates... through the magical door of this festival... a blanket in hand to lay claim to a spot that would become our chosen garden so that these memories could grow and our hearts could sing...

and as we sat and listened... Utah Phillip's white beard and chosen words can no longer be seen or heard...yet he touched our souls deeply with his tales and songs... his philosophy of life... times that are lost as the railroads have changed, and with this change a silence came... and now only his chosen words told of the struggles he faced... the battles that were fought, and the friends that were made along that endless road...

and to the grandchildren of Pete Seeger and Woody Guthrie who too are blessed with the voice of their elders... they now walk down a well-traveled road touching the spirits of many… and for the smile from Woody Guthrie' son Arlo as he glances at his children, Abe and Sarah… they too now stand upon a wooden stage and as he and his father did to sing the past and current songs of change… do they know their father's pride… can Arlo sense their happiness to share in his endless road of dreams…

i wonder with envy at the countless evenings where song and the gentle strums from a wooden guitar were shared… they sat …listening… lost in their own dreams of years yet to be… and of that special time when in their youth… the small hands of a child would play with their father's guitar… and as he patiently taught them the ballet their hands would perform on that wooden guitar… and over the many evenings the countless words were learned…and to their father's tears of joy as he sees his father's legacy continue… and to know that the words of his children's children will continue the painting of so many hearts with hope and song…

and for the countless times…. my sister and i each casting a glance to the other… if only for a moment… a smile or a tear in our eyes because for that precious moment our hearts are both being deeply touched by the voices from those small wooden stages… and to the endless times… we too joined in spirit and lifted our voices out loud and sang as they said "there is never a wrong note in a song that is song from your heart"…and we cared not, for these troubadours gave us these special moments that we shared in part with…

Tranquility Days

i had just bought Tranquility, a 30' Catalina Tall Rig Sloop, a few weeks earlier, and was now done teaching for the school year... i was driving to San Diego to spend the first of many days and weeks on...

May 31, 2004
On board Tranquility
Marina Cortez, San Diego

it's dark outside and i'm safely tucked down in the cabin of Tranquility, a dream come true... the smell of salt air hangs heavy in the damp air... the gulls are quiet and only the slight slapping of water against Tranquility's hull can be heard... the past few days have been an adventure in boat ownership and maintenance... Jeffrey, my brother and an excellent shipwright, has been constantly on my mind as i call out," Jeff where are you when i need you"... slowly and by asking hundreds of questions i'm learning... the pages from my small library of books on boat and diesel engine maintenance are being turned often... now with an endless list of should-do, must-do, would-be-nice-to-do, and someday-i'll-do jobs, i have more than enough to keep me busy... but in this moment i sit in silence and listen to the soft sounds of the night...

after repeatedly referring to my notes and my engine manual i was finally able to start Tranquility's engine for the first time yet i journeyed nowhere; nevertheless, this was an enormous first step for me...

long ago, when i was working on my very first boat, the boat my grandfather bought me, he provided me with my first life-long lesson on boats... he told me that if i treat my boat like a beautiful

181

lady, that lady will always take care of me… so ever so slowly, in these first few days, as i learn my way around Tranquility, i am learning how to treat this beautiful lady of mine… i will cherish her and treat her tenderly and lovingly, for in my heart i know she will sail me into many dreams… David Crosby wrote a song, *The Lee Shore*, about his love affair with Mayan, his wooden schooner… i haven't written my song yet to Tranquility, but i am falling deeply in love with her…

during my days i often find my eyes looking south towards Pt. Loma and the ocean… i must be patient, for my time will come… a time when i will finally unfurl Tranquility's sails, and feel the wind fill her sails as she takes possession of my heart as we both sail away… treat her like a lady i will…

to you Joanne, my wife and best friend, i owe this dream to you… but not only of Tranquility but of this life i have shared with you…

> and i love you
> till forever's come and gone
> till the day i die
> till the sun's gone

Mason Proffit

June 2, 2004
Marina Cortez, San Diego
(from Tranquility's Log)
Sky Conditions: clear with scattered clouds Wind: NE @ 10 kts
Destination: San Diego Bay/ Richie and Chris aboard

(from Tranquility's journal)
i left the dock for the first time… taking my brother's advice, i realized the key to backing out of the slip was to go as slow as possible but never forget that without speed you will never have steerage… i backed out having her stern going to the starboard then

cutting power and letting her motion carry me completely out before putting the motor in gear while turning to the port and proceeding out the marina…

(from Tranquility's log)
cruised at 4 knots for about an hour… motored down San Diego Bay to the carrier U.S. Midway then returned to the dock… GPS registered 6 knots with the engine's gauges reading 2500 RPM, engine temperature steady at 180^0

(from Tranquility's Journal)
for the first time i left the safety of the dock and ventured toward San Diego Bay… a thousand things constantly running through my mind… failure always on my mind… constantly wishing my brother Jeff was here to coach me… Jeff's words of advice to go as slow as you can… once i completely backed out of my slip and headed out of the marina i felt so proud of my accomplishment… it may have looked like nothing to anyone on the dock watching… a maneuver that took place a hundred times a day but for me this was my first, and the first is always the hardest… my celebration was the fact that i did it… heading out towards the bay, i stood as the captain of my vessel behind the helm of my lady, Tranquility… it doesn't get any better than this… today my journey was small, more important than the destination… destinations will come later but i will always remember and cherish this small journey

June 4, 2004
Marina Cortez, San Diego… on board Tranquility
(from Tranquility's Journal)
today i spent re-plumbing all my water lines on Tranquility… i spent a good part of yesterday identifying and figuring out the fresh and salt water flow of water… i talked to my brother Jeff again yesterday and he told me to mark all the lines as either fresh or salt water and also the direction of flow… Jeff also strongly suggested that i replace all the hoses as i have no idea how old any of the lines are… part of the day was spent running back and forth to West Marina or Home

Depot... i'm learning real quick that anything that is marked as marine is more expensive... Jeff told me to get all the hoses at Home Depot as all the tubing will be the same regardless where i buy it, but Home Depot is a lot cheaper... also it seems with every little job i'm doing i'm running over to Harbor Tools to buy another tool for my toolbox...

as i was working on Tranquility's water system i could feel the constant presence of my grandfather reminding me to "treat her like a lady" but more importantly to do the job right... i imagined him looking over my shoulder, pointing his screwdriver at me telling me to do it over as it wasn't right... it's funny but Jeff always did everything right in my grandfather's eyes, and i always seemed to have some issues going on... "he's a little slow" would often be heard from my grandfather, but regardless, i loved my grandfather for all he taught me...

part of yesterday and today i worked on scrubbing the name off of Tranquility's hull... the previous owner did a crappy job hand painting the name, Tranquility, on the hull and i want the job done right with the name professionally put on the stern and both the port and starboard sides of the hull... when i signed the papers buying Tranquility i put in the paperwork to have Tranquility a Documented Vessel by the U.S. Coast Guard... every documented boat must also have a Hailing Port that it is registered in... as long as the U.S. location has a zip code it will qualify as a hailing port even though it's not on a coast... Tranquility will be hailing now out of Audubon, New Jersey... i grew up on 224 Walnut St., Audubon, New Jersey... i always felt that was the one childhood house i had the most connection with

June 6, 2004
Marina Cortez, San Diego... aboard Tranquility
(from Tranquility's Log)
Sky Conditions: hazy with overcast stratus clouds Wind: SSW @ 12 kts. Destination: San Diego Bay

motored out of Marina Cortez and once i passed the buoys restricting speed, i turned Tranquility into the wind and raised her main sail and let out the jib sail… sailed down to the carrier Midway several times varying from a Beam Reach to a Close Haul… encountered several problems, mainly on learning which sheet goes to what sail… i did not release the Down Haul after i raised the sail then tighten it prior to lowering the sail… real problems with the jib furling as it got twisted and then wouldn't roll back in again… once i started back to the marina i motored in with the jib hand tied as best we could… talking to other sailboat owners they gave me a name of a Rigger who would be able to fix it…

(from Tranquility's Journal)
today i let the wind fill Tranquility's sail… once i turned away from the wind i heard a beautiful whoosh as the wind filled her sails… all at once she heeled over on her side as the water raced madly by her hull… while wrapping the jib sheet around the winch i could hear the strain being placed on the rigging… with the sound of the wind and water this had to be the most beautiful feeling i could imagine… and in that moment i knew i was forever addicted to sailing… the journey was small but that wasn't important, the important fact was my lady's sails had wind in them and we were sailing… at times i would look up at her beautiful white sails, filled with the wind, against a beautiful blue sky knowing a dream had finally come true… the joy and happiness that filled me, i can't describe… standing at her helm and feeling the wind in my face made me feel like a million dollars… how many silent prayers of thanks i whispered…

June 8, 2004
Marina Cortez, San Diego… aboard Tranquility
(from Tranquility's Journal)
this was another first that took place… today i had to take Tranquility over to Shelter Island to have a rigger look at the jib furling… i was alone now, with no one to offer advice or lend a

hand as i very slowly backed out of the slip… to say i was nervous is an understatement but with Jeff's spirit with me, encouraging me along, i had to believe if i did everything slowly, all would go right… motoring over to Shelter Island in the early morning it was quiet on the water with a very slight breeze… throughout my small journey i kept worrying how i would possibly parallel park a boat along the repair dock… but with Tranquility holding my hand she made me proud, or was it simply the dock hand assisting me… nevertheless, i eventually had Tranquility secured along the dock… i'm beginning to realize that it's these small fragments of minutes that are starting to form memories that will last a lifetime… thank you Jeff for your inspiration and encouragement… and i long to sail away with my 2 brothers with our laughter echoing in the wind…

June 9, 2004
Marina Cortez, San Diego… aboard Tranquility
(from Tranquility's Journal)

to Tranquility, my lady of the islands
and i hear your silent whispers
calling
calling to my soul,
your lingering scent
stirs these restless blues…
m'lady i'm traveling home to you.

hold my hand and sail we will
sail me away to hear the mermaids sing
the blowing of the whales
the cries of the gulls
just hold this soul
carefree and drifting with the wind
m'lady i'm sailing with you.

m'lady take me to the horizons

where the evening sun sets,
far, far away
where the scent of this troubled land is no more…
let me witness the sun rising
a new day dawning with prayers for fair winds
the soaring of an albatross
m'lady i'm sailing with you.

m'lady take me away
to feel your gentle rhythms
lose my soul where time doesn't matter
and the flooding of the tides can't be felt
only the wind that fills your sails…
and with my worn and soiled charts
a star as my compass
take me away m'lady
sailing away with you

jtalarico

June 10, 2004
Marina Cortez, San Diego… aboard Tranquility
(from Tranquility's Journal)

a CSN tape is playing while the sun sinks below the horizon bringing my 55th birthday slowly to a close…

today was a special day as Tranquility's birthday present to me was a beautiful mid-day sail around San Diego Bay… with a gentle breeze on my face, Tranquility slipped gracefully through the waters as the gulls circled above, their cries, music to my ears … i stood proudly at the helm; the captain with a beautiful lady holding his hand… looking up at the beauty of her billowing white sail, the wind sculpting it into perfection against a cloudless blue sky… time and time again i would remember this lady was mine, a young boy's dream finally being fulfilled… i wished my mother and father could have seen their son now, their beautiful gift given to this world, and the happiness that filled his soul… i thank you again mom, for it was you who gave me this special gift, my love for the sea, and like your brother, my eyes shine the brightest when the sea is in their reflection…

my time with Tranquility this past week and a half has been a dream come true… Joanne i miss you dearly, but being on Tranquility has been so special; it's a love affair forming, and she is quickly stealing my heart… i'm slowly beginning to realize what my future will be like next year… i can't wait to retire, to enjoy this new stage of my life… thinking of my father, who died years before he was scheduled to retire… he often talked of those days to be, yet sadly they never came… i feel guilty thinking of my retirement with Joanne just a year away, a gift that was denied to my father… i will never understand God's ways, the reason why my father had to die so young and with so much pain… an endless loneliness my mother must live with… His work is a mystery and i pray to understand…

but tonight i'll dream of looking upward at that beautiful white sail, with the wind in my face and my lady dancing upon the waves, realizing she is mine to treasure in the days to be… thank you Joanne, and i love you, till forever come and goes, till the day i die, till the sun's gone…

June 15, 2004
Marina Cortez

night is slowing fading in… the wind has picked up considerably, possibly due to a storm moving in… once again i find myself in my little corner of Tranquility's cabin sitting on the settee, a book laying by my side… i listen to the rigging whistling in the wind and feel the strain of the docking lines holding us secure… my kerosene lamp swings rhythmically like the pendulum of a clock as my last evening on Tranquility slips away…

these past 18 days have been beautiful… my hands are sore and calloused from the hours of work… my body tanned from the sun and i sit here now with mixed feelings on leaving… our journeys were few but they provided me with mountains of dreams and fond memories… i know with each trip we will venture further towards my first sail out past Pt. Loma and into the Pacific…

but i am anxious to feel Joanne's arms around me again… my name being called sweetly from her lips … i think, will my heart always be torn as to which lady will be my reflection… but i know these two ladies will always hold me dearly and let me dream…

and to Tranquility, my thoughts will always have you in them, yes m'lady of my islands wait patiently for i'll return to you with the wind…

Hello Again My Friend
November 30, 2013

                a motel just outside the Park boundary i stand in an empty stillness close to the canyon's edge and stare out into a cold emptiness… a thick fog blankets the canyon causing its pallet of colors to be…

erased and hidden… a silence, that's hard to describe, fills the air… i am cold and want to get warm but i cannot walk away… the canyon's spirit has grabbed me once again as a barrage of emotions pound my thoughts and soul… it has been at least 20 years since i have stood at this canyon's edge… i was younger then… years ago, this journey i will take in the morning would have been just another hike, for i have hiked this trail and this canyon countless times before… but 20 years has slowing slipped by… i am restless…

December 1, 2013
Written in Bright Angel Campground
after my hike into the canyon.

i stayed in a hotel room for the night thinking back to those many canyon trips when the night before i would have been in my tent in a campground regardless of the weather… have i aged that much… i slept restless throughout the night… constantly thinking about, and possibly even fearing, the long hike that awaited… would my boots carry me as they did in my youth… i would find out soon enough…

in the early hours of dawn, hungry yet restless, with the canyon close by, i packed my backpack… it was cold and my hands were stiff as i started a ritual i had done so many times before… but now the task was awkward even though this backpack was the same that i carried for many years… still stained with the sweat from countless miles and journeys… i had to remember how i organized my pack… the little places my necessities were stashed , even the order i loaded my backpack… so many years have slipped by… i finally stashed my water bottle and some snacks for later feeling confident that i was ready for what awaited… securing my backpack i walked slowly, maybe hesitating with doubt, but still anxious to prove my strength and skills had not weathered away… standing at the trailhead, cold and restless i began my hike… it always begins with that first step, and after i took that step i knew it would feel good to carry this friend , my backpack, on my back once again, on a trail my boots knew know so well…

it's cloudy and cold… i'm in my tent… sheltered and with a warm mug of tea… yes i'm deep within the canyon… alone with only my thoughts… a flood of distant canyon memories and the night chill are my only companions… it's been a long time since i slept within this canyon and in these moments my heart knows it has been much too long…

but then i had my years of kayaking… years of following the whales… all of this cemented the ocean as a long lost friend i had missed dearly… and these years and journeys eventually led me to Tranquility, my beloved Catalina 30-foot sailboat… for 11 years i filled her sails with the wind… years i hold so dear as they were a young man's dream… they were good years… years in which i painted my life with so many rich memories… memories i carry with me today… yet this friend of mine, the canyon, patiently waited for me to return… as i stood at the trailhead just yesterday, the canyon was still covered by a thick cloud, but it didn't matter as i didn't have to see its many shades of colors… i have been such a part of this canyon that i could never forget its face… i knew what awaited me… the trail was the same… only i had changed… you may say i've been weathered… my steps were slower yet my eyes were alive as i was excited to see this friend's face once again… my boots took my hands and slowly led me on this journey…

as i descended into the canyon, i was flooded with memories from my past… it was 33 years ago this month when i took this same trail to lay my father's ashes to rest within the canyon that he loved… i remembered his excitement as we rode the mules down into the canyon… a dream of his that his son gave to him… countless times, as i hiked this trail, my hands always touching the rocks, repeating the canyon's story to myself or to others… funny, i still love to touch the rocks and smell that earthly scent… it's a good smell… an honest smell… slowly, as i walked within the depth of this canyon, the fog began to thin and the beauty of the canyon unfolded… the trail, as usual, was never ending as it continued downward… i thought, was it always this steep or have i grown softer with age… the downward descent was taking its toll on my knees… the rock layers slowly passed by… the viewpoint at Cedar Ridge… i remember that spot like it was yesterday, but my father's image no longer filled the frame… he had his cigar and wore my blue down vest, the one i still wear to this day… memories painfully faded away… downward, always downward i hiked… the countless switchbacks of the Redwall Limestone… my knees recorded each and every one of those switchbacks… finally the Tonto platform opened before me and revealed the point from which i released my father's ashes… i stopped as the memories were good but painful… so many years ago and my tears still found their way down my face… the descent into the gorge was rough… my knees were feeling their age… i walked ever so slowly now when years ago my pace would have quickened as i knew i was almost to the river… finally i stood at the bridge and looked out on the river… my eyes searching for an old lost friend… yes it was still there, the rock that i sat upon so many times in the past… the river has changed and now my rock sits too far from the bank to sit upon… but it remains and that was all that was important…

later that day i wandered down to Phantom Ranch… bitter sweet memories flooded my thoughts… it was in a small cabin in this campground that my father and i shared during that trip… i will never forget the love and excitement in his eyes… his dream was now his reality… i tried to recall the talks my father and i shared, the quiet moments… but the pages of time have worn those memories thin… but as i looked at the small cabins, others now sat by them maybe enjoying their dreams… i will never forget how special those moments that…shared were to each of us… today my walk within Phantom Ranch had no real destination… i stopped at the corral where our mules were tied and there was the sign "Phantom Ranch Welcomes You"… regardless how hard i tried my father's images were gone from under that sign… all i have left is the framed photo of that moment that hangs in my study… Phantom Ranch was filled with so many memories from that journey… the lodge where we ate… how my father talked so proudly of his son over that bowl of stew…all those memories, so many memories… i wandered alone back to my empty tent with tears in my heart…

December 2, 2013

Bright Angel Campground

Written at home after driving back from the Grand Canyon i tossed and turned throughout the night… about 1a.m. i forced myself to leave the warmth of my sleeping bag and get up to do my nightly ritual… quickly throwing on some warm clothes, i left my tent to be greeted by an incredible night sky… it was beautiful outside… the night air was cold and the sky was ablaze with a thousand different stars bordered by the dark silhouette of the canyon walls… i stood transfixed… how long i stood there i really don't know, but it was cold… i wanted to return to the warmth of my awaiting sleeping bag, yet i stood there transfixed staring at the stars against the silhouette of the canyon…

my morning came early… it was still dark outside as i went through the ritual of tearing down my tent and repacking my pack… my morning mug of Tang warmed me while thoughts of my long hike to the rim ran through my mind… it was only roughly a six and a half mile hike to the south rim… a hike i have done countless times in the past… i remember how it was always a challenge to see if i could break the four hour time of my fastest hike to the rim… today my thoughts were simply just making it to the rim in one piece… oatmeal was made with my granola and honey… some habits will never change… eventually it was time to lace up my friends and strap on my pack…

i left in solitude just as i arrived… i stopped once again at the bridge and said good-bye to my boulder… a sentinel in the river, guarding the passage of time and always being cleansed by the river… throughout my hike i repeated the old hiker's prayer, "Lord if you pick them up… i'll put them down" (referring to my feet)… switchback after switchback, baby steps, one in front of the other… slowly, very slowly the miles wore away… the inner gorge, the Tapeat Sandstone… a brief goodbye to the site of my father's ashes… the Tonto, the trail climbed steadily… i knew once i had the Redwall Limestone behind me, the worst would be over… one step followed by another and another… the sequence going on in what felt like an eternity… i was proud of my ascent as these weathered legs still have a lot of life in them… my boots carried me onward… my stride was feeling the weight from my pack… baby steps…"pick them up Lord and i'll put them down"… then almost too soon the end was in sight… and with that i knew my journey would soon be over… too tired to linger and ponder on my journey i simply let my boots take me the final steps to the rim… it was a good walk… thank you God…

Ode to a Forgotten God

Historical Note

Glacial Bay was created by the Grand Pacific Glacier. Margerie, Johns Hopkins, Lamplugh, and all the other glaciers in the park were tributaries that eventually fed into the Grand Pacific Glacier. In 1797 when Captain Vancouver sailed eastward in Icy Straits, there was no Glacial Bay; instead, there was the face of the Grand Pacific Glacier. Tlingit stories tell us that prior to 1600 AD the face of the Grand Pacific stood north of Barlett Cove, somewhere between Willoughby Island and Strawberry Island. Then during the northern hemisphere's Little Ice Age that lasted from roughly 1350 AD to 1850 AD, the Grand Pacific Glacier started to advance and reached its southern limit in Icy Straits. As the Little Ice Age ended, the glacier began its long retreat. In 1897 when John Muir visited Glacier Bay, it had receded north to near Russell Island. Today, over 200 years since Vancouver sailed through Icy Straits, the Grand Pacific Glacier has retreated over 60 miles and now rests on solid ground, no longer a tidewater glacier.

Aug 4, 2014

Ode to a Forgotten God

all eyes were drawn to Margerie Glacier, and it's no wonder with its glacial face painted in of shades of white and blue, rested in the icy waters of Glacier Bay… towers of ice stood in silent testimony to your glacial dance and awaited their eventual fate… all cameras were aimed and all stood and waited patiently… a stillness painted this moment of time… one could feel the anticipation that filled the air as passengers awaited the crack of white thunder… then in the seconds that followed, all eyes frantically searched for your calving… but not i, for i stood alone in thought as i looked at the Grand Pacific Glacier…

it was in another lifetime… all eyes were drawn to you… you were not old and worn but young and strong… today you are tired, and you are covered with the scars of age and slowly, ever so slowly, you are drifting from our sight… i stand here alone in your company as all eyes are not on you, and i wonder whether they know you lie here at all… and i think of a time in your youth when all we now admire was covered and hidden because of your restless spirit… no one knew of the beauty that you would create under your icy skin…

at first, all they could do was to sail quietly by… this wilderness did not yet exist, for you stood guardian over the entrance to this bay, a barrier not even the gods could penetrate… yet it was only several generations ago from that day that they sailed by that stories were told… stories from many a voices that are now silent and gone… stories that were passed to those that were so much younger and not as wise… the stories told of your restless spirit and how you came alive and how you danced with a winter wind onward, and nothing, nothing could stop you… stories have been passed down of the day they had to flee from the flooding of your tide for you now silently controlled their lives… yes, you were young and strong…

and many a summers passed before a wise one came and fell in love with your spirit… he touched your soul during many travels and spoke often of your beauty… your name today was given by him and i wonder what he thought of you, that day that your name was first heard from his lips… and in a way it was because of him that we too took this journey, but we do not kneel at your alter in praise as he did…

time has etched its mark on your tired spirit, my friend… but even though you are leaving us and your blue spirit is faded and covered with time, i will stand alone today and sing your praises… old friends should never be left alone and their names should still be echoed in this wilderness… today i choose to walk away from the crowds that look elsewhere and i remember how i stood in silence and uttered a silent prayer for you my friend… my friend, you will not be forgotten…

jtalarico

Selling Tranquility

Tranquility's Last Entries in Her Logbook
life is full of many journeys… some you really never want to end,
but like all journeys they have an ending… my journey with
Tranquility will always be cherished… these words are taken from
my final entries in her Ship's Log… after i sold Tranquility i kept her
Logbook and Ensign… today i still hold these treasures so dear…

November 11, 2014
Call it what you want… a new chapter… a beginning… moving on,
or the end of a beautiful relationship… it really doesn't matter what
i call this, but i must walk this troubled path… i will walk it alone,
with much thought, turmoil, and definitely regret…

i finally made the decision to put Tranquility, a dream come
true, up for sale… was it time… i really thought it was, but i would
be lying if i said i didn't have second thoughts…

when i returned from Alaska, to check on the main sail's
condition after a long summer of not being used, i was frustrated
with the constant pain in my elbow… i could barely raise the main
sail to check on its condition… my body was now plagued with pain
in everything i tried to do…when i tried to pull out her batteries and
check them, the task was almost too much for me…

this was the first summer that passed without beautiful days
spent sailing or just being with my lady… Alaska was calling me
away during the summer months more and more… within a year
she would need a new mainsail and jib, her bottom paint needed to
be redone which meant having her taken out of the water, and i
needed to address issues with her rudder… these needs would easily
be $20,000… money that i would never be able to recover when i
eventually sold her… Tranquility was in good selling condition now,
so i do needed to take advantage of that fact…

i can read through the pages that make up this journal, her ship's log, a log and journal that i kept from the first day i boarded her… God how i wish i had that first day back again… the excitement… the future filled with so many dreams… i was blessed, for by reading these pages, i am able to relive a dream i thought i would never have… this has been a beautiful journey and i thank God every day for it…

slowly over the course of 2 days i filled boxes with what made Tranquility special to me, what made Tranquility, Tranquility… it was the little things that brought the tears… with each item i packed away i remembered the occasion when i found that special gift… in all my travels, to famous ports around the world, i always brought a token of gratitude back from the port of call i was visiting to decorate her with… i can remember making the decision that this would be the perfect touch for my lady… hurrying back to Tranquility to give her my gifts… gifts that were today to be found throughout her beautiful cabin… the Captain name plate that was mounted over my berth… the oil lantern that gave me a warm glow during all those lonely evenings in which we shared a treasured solitude… boxes were filled with memories that can never, and will never, be taken from me… i still took the time to carefully wash her down, i always wanted my lady to look beautiful… oh how i'll miss all the hours of tinkering, of caring, caressing and always admiring with pride… as the boxes were finally being filled, i witnessed her spirit slowly fade away… what made her mine was packed away in those boxes… i knew the hardest part was yet to come… finally i made that emotional phone call and told my yacht broker to list Tranquility for sale…

i left Tranquility that weekend knowing that different hands would be looking after her in the future… would they ever be able to see or even feel the love and joy she gave back to me…
some roads are hard to walk… i know this road will be one… ah my little lady, my Tranquility… oh God how i love you so…

December 17, 2014

a phone call… words were spoken… and with those words my dream came to an end… yes, Tranquility was sold. should i be happy… no instead i shed a silent tear as i felt my heart breaking as my dream really started coming to its end… dreams are beautiful things in life… they can keep your spirit alive… they are a form of hope for the future… yet dreams have to end

it's hard to imagine my life without Tranquility… she was a life's dream… part of my daily thoughts… something i always looked forward to… those quiet moments we shared… i hated to think that i would not hear the wind fill her sails… feel her hull heeled over with the ocean racing by… the salt air in my face… beautiful moments that became memories that i will always cherish…

i still have yet one more trip to take… after i filled more boxes and removed all my tools, foul weather gear, and the few clothes i left, i still had to take my final sail, her sea trial with her new owner… i flew her ensign as i always did, but accepted the fact that now new hands would replace the movements that had always been mine… i will have to step away from the helm that for so many hours my hands held onto… always guiding her along… the compass… how many times was my course checked looking at that compass… my eyes never grew tired from her reflection… i reverently shed a light on her personality… how she liked her sails to be trimmed… revealed her soul and spirit… i must let her go… but i will with a prayer of thanks…

December 26, 2014

it's night now… the marina is quiet… the air outside is cool and soon i will have to turn on my little space heater… like so many other evenings when i sat in this spot, music filled the cabin… yet as i look around i see only empty shadows of what once was my dream… all that made Tranquility mine, my books, my treasures, they have all been taken off… i sit alone without even Joshua, my dog and sailing companion, to keep my tears company… he should be here with me… his blue pillow that spent many a days on my berth has been packed away… his reflection is gone… there will be no more long walks along the bay with him by my side… those lazy mornings with the two of us, sitting in the cockpit, reading, just enjoying the moment… as i look through my tears i see so many beautiful memories that were made… this boat is a treasure chest filled with memories that are only mine… it's sad but nobody really knows of my time with Tranquility… all the memories will be lost with me…

tomorrow i'll do the "sea trial"… meet the new hands that will caress my lady… i can only pray that they treat her as i did…
i feel so empty tonight… i want to just curl up in my berth and cry to sleep… but my time is so limited… in a way i wanted the night to last forever… she was still mine and i can't think of leaving her…

December 27, 2014
Day of Tranquility's Sea Trial

it's a beautiful day today… blue skies with the promise of wind…

today will most likely be my last sail on Tranquility… a thought that i had a hard time really grasping… my feelings are numb… my emotions are drained… my tears are dry and gone… i cannot even think about what my emotions, my thoughts will be when her sails are raised… no longer raised by my hands, with my eyes lifted upward… watching that beautiful white sail as it reaches for the heavens… and then when the engine goes silent and the wind fills her sails and i hear her rigging being strained as she heels over and the water rushes by her hull… will this also be witnessed by her new owner… i know there will be many a secret tears shed in the day ahead…

but for now i sit alone… alone with a million memories in a spot i have sat so many times before… and this morning i sit here and have my last mug of tea aboard Tranquility… as i sit here i only wish i could grab a hold and relive each and every one of those golden and salty memories… and Joshua… he was my faithful first mate… he should be here with me… he always wanted and hoped to jump up on my lap and be a part of the minutes we spent with my lady

i left the dock for the last time… i was glad i was alone with my tears… i would meet the hands that would care for Tranquility over on Shelter Island… so this last journey i took slowly as my tears would not let the minutes rush by… how many times i traveled these waters only to wait for the wind… a day on the water… what could possibly be better… but today was so different…

i waited on a foreign dock… numb… i hate these minutes…

finally, and for my very last time i guided Tranquility from its berth… and then i handed her helm to new hands… God i pray they will cherish this dream… we sailed the bay… words were said but i heard but a few… i was lost in sadness… so many times i wanted my hands to take the helm again… i cursed my decision to let her go… must this beautiful dream end… finally as i knew my last minutes were racing by i took the helm for the last time… i felt her ways… was she also shedding tears as we parted our ways… slowly i took her to the dock…

many words were said and broken promises were made… her name will no longer grace her sides as her new owner didn't like the name Tranquility… in a way i'm happy because Tranquility was me… we were one for all those years… soulmates…

and then i was alone… i packed my bags and loaded the dock cart… the minutes raced by slowly… i hesitated a million times… i looked time and time again with my hungry eyes as i wanted to capture every image and thought for an eternity… i left her cabin only to return again… my tears were my only companion along with my broken heart… i locked her companionway… and then i walked silently away… i looked back countless times as my dream came crashing to a close… a final photo… my final steps as i walked out of a beautiful dream…

January 9, 2015

papers were signed… there was no excitement like the last time… no anxious dreams of the days ahead… i moved reluctantly through the motions knowing it was all but gone… were these my betrayal papers… and my bag of silver… they were just coins… coins that anyone could gather… and with these papers my name and her's were gone… erased… no longer spoken… no longer your name would be heard… i was so sorry for what i had done… the tears i shed were endless… they represented our love… all those magical days we shared… God what have i done… i walked away… but before i left i knew that i loved her so very much… and always… always i knew i would have our memories that i will cherish… Tranquility… you always will be a beautiful dream that i loved so very much…

thank you… and to you, Joanne… my eternal thanks for giving me a dream…

January 14, 2015

the last entry in Tranquility's log

i held a check in my hand… but in my heart i held memories of a dream that lasted for 11 years… to me they were worth more than this bag of tarnished silver…

a year later these words were penned…
and i cry
i cry for those tranquility days are gone
damn it, why did i let them slip away in the night…
do we ever know our blessings until they are stolen
from our grasp…
you tell me there are others to be had
the hell with you

for i will never be able to replace perfection
she was mine
and she's gone
god i love… no i hate these memories…
does the pain of loss feel good
does it bronze those lost memories forever

Aleutian Ballad

Late January or within

the first few days of February 2016

the phone rang and to my surprise i heard the voice of Derrick… Derrick is an Alaskan commercial fishermen, whom i met several summers ago, on a Princess Cruise excursion on the Aleutian Ballad in Ketchikan, Alaska… "hey jules, do you want to go crabbing, if so, get your butt up here in a week, as we're taking the Aleutian Ballad back up to Ketchikan to do some crabbing for Alaskan king crabs"… without even hesitating, i said yes… as i hung up the phone i couldn't believe what just transpired, i would be standing side by side with commercial crabbers who spent their life crabbing in the Bering Sea… i would help take the Aleutian Ballad, the famous crabbing boat, from season two of The Deadliest Catch, back up to Alaska… the Ballad became world known because while crabbing in the Bering Sea it was hit by a rogue wave and survived a winter storm… the whole scenario was captured on film and seen on television's Discovery Channel, with the series, The Deadliest Catch… today the Ballad is a tourist attraction and used by the cruising industry as an Alaskan excursion in Ketchikan, Alaska… all through the previous summer i hinted to Derrick to take me with them the following winter as they caught their load of king crabs that would last them throughout the tourist summer… well i guess it all paid out, because immediately my bags were packed, an airline flight scheduled, and i flew to Portland, Oregon, to meet Derrick, Andy, and Terry to take the Ballad up to Alaska…

Feb 11, 2016

Sharing the 4 o'clock watch in the

pilot house of the Ballad with Derrick

i was once again at sea… we left in the darkness of night, in a light

204

rain, with a flood tide that took the waters of the Columbia River out to the Pacific Ocean… an hour later, with a slack tide (a slack tide is when the tidal strength is at its lowest and therefore safer for navigation) we crossed, without incident, the famous and treacherous Columbia River Bar, and headed towards the open ocean… a journey i talked about all last summer… a journey that jules always wanted to take… it was in the darkness of an early dawn and the rain was still falling… the sea seemed to be alive as the swells gradually built and started to push us around quite a bit… the wind was blowing at 20 kts, yet i was protected as i sat in the pilot house, both safe and warm… i sat in the helm chair, on the port side of the pilot house; Derrick was piloting from the starboard side… in the background was the steady hum of the engines that slowly pushed us northward… we were still off the coast of Washington, on a course that would take us north of Vancouver Island…. the rain continued to fall as my thoughts wandered back to my time with Tranquility… i truly missed my little lady… a dream that lived for 11 beautiful years until i sold her and walked away from her one evening last January… today my heart still cried, as it was the hardest goodbye i ever had to do… i often wonder where my lady is today… are hands like mine tenderly caressing her every day… i miss her scent… i miss her touch… i miss her being… as is so often the case with boats, i sold her not because i wanted to, but because i had to balance the financial needs of the present against future expenses— new sails, new rudder, new paint… $20,000 in expenses that i would never be able to recover…

i sat and watched the constant rain and the flight of the gulls… carefree, we moved with the winds… i kept looking to the east as i awaited the dawn of this new day while the rain continued to fall…

Feb 12, 2016
Somewhere off the coast of British Columbia

and the rain continued to fall as i thought back to yesterday… i wondered did the rain ever stop… once again it was in the quiet hours of predawn… the world was dark and silent, the wind and the sea could not be felt or heard… slowly this island that i floated upon moved ever northward… silently the wind and currents pushed us towards Alaska… i was at peace, in that moment, for the sea had always brought me peace… the steady rhythm of the swells… the rain against the glass that i stared out through to a cold distant world… the marine radio broke the silence with an advisory of a distant storm… i thought, will the fury of an ocean storm finally be felt, but our journey took us safely to the north of this storm…

i wondered and i prayed… can't my mind just rest… shut out my tormented thoughts of the world i would have to live within because of words i said… these moments, on the sea with friends, will also soon be lost, only to be relived through my memory… and so i closed my eyes while the hours silently and peacefully passed by… i was on the sea, the sea that was in my blood, the sea that i loved…

later as i sat there, i looked across the pilot house… there sat my friend Derrick… we first ran across each other several years ago as fate took our separate paths and allowed them to cross and a beautiful friendship to form… over the many months that have slipped by, there have been many laughs and good times… will i have to say goodbye to this friend… paths cross, but then diverge as life's journeys onward, and the journey i will soon have to take, will it take us down different roads… because of this friend, i sat here fulfilling another dream…this trip allowed me to see this ocean that i loved from the eyes of a commercial fisherman…

i cried into this rain as i thought, will this also now be lost with what lies ahead for me… could Derrick even begin to understand what pain and frustration can lead one to do, what i must do… the journey i must take… this trip was becoming another wake-up call for how my future will be scarred by this life-changing journey that i began just a few months ago…

Feb 13, 2016

still off the coast of British Columbia

the rain continued to fall… i sat once again and looked out at a world of wind, rain and swells… it seemed we left Astoria at the right time as we were staying ahead of the worst of the weather… yesterday afternoon there were small windows of sunshine but mostly we have been accompanied by gray skies and rain… i felt a chill in the air that was not here before as we headed further north … the temperature will probably continue to drop as we head further north towards my beloved town of Ketchikan, but for the rest of today, the swells and wind continued to push us northward while this rain continued to wash our pallet…

being on this journey upon the sea i found there were many idle moments that allowed my mind to drift like the currents… at times i thought of my past… my many journeys that this soul of mine had experienced and as i meditated on each of those journeys… i wondered did i really know the course i was taking through life… i felt most of the time i was just caught in the flood or ebb of the tides of my life… did i really know my true destination… with each summit that i reached there was always a moment of idle satisfaction… i reflected over what was accomplished and also i stared hard into the unknown future… yes, there were always the deep valleys that i descended into… and at times it grew dark and i felt lost… my course felt uncertain… was there always a plan that was carefully laid out… i thought not, but i always set a course with my compass and seemed to move ahead…

but am i moving ahead now… i felt caught in a riptide of emotions… pulling me every which way… i fought to rise above this water that i felt was trying to drown me… yes, i do know what i want to do… i have waited a lifetime and fought through many a storms, but i cried and wondered why the winds of mixed emotions formed into still one more storm of doubt… was fate trying to change my course… i cried in confusion… i knew the pain of one course… i lived through its pain and its joy… and of this new course that i have just barely touched… its joys brought smiles that i never had but i am so afraid of its pain…

Feb 14, 2016

Ketchikan, Alaska

it was late last night, as a gentle rain fell, that i saw the lights of Ketchikan once again… i was back in my beloved Ketchikan… a thousand memories does this small town hold… there were my walks, rainy days with a thousand puddles that my boots played within… it felt good to be back in my Alaskan home… only the noise from the bars was heard from the docks, as the streets were empty of the thousands of tourists who wandered about in search of their Alaskan memories… i often wondered what memories of Alaska they took back home with them, were they just the t-shirts and jewelry that would eventually be lost over their empty years…
a gentle winter rain was washing away, yet another day… it washed away the stains left from those crowds… for tonight the streets belonged to those whose songs are heard from the many bars… the docks were empty and stood silent, so beautiful without the ships that came every year with the summer rains to haunt this little pocket of Alaskan paradise… yes it felt good to be home once again…

i enjoyed this time on the Ballad with these friends… our laughter and talks… the moments that words did not have to be spoken as we watched the sea cast its many shadows as we slowly headed north… sitting around the Ballad's small table, gypsies of the sea, we shared meals and listen to stories and laughed throughout the night… i now felt a tear of sadness as thoughts of tomorrow grow near… no matter the path i walk there was going to be pain… how was i to choose the path, for no matter which journey i choose, there will also be tears…

Feb 15, 2016
Preparing to go crabbing for
Alaskan King Crabs

today my friends wore the reflection of a life they have loved and lived for most of their lives… they are the commercial fishermen that i often wished i had been, but little did i know the work that was involved to bear the title of a commercial fishermen… as soon as their feet hit the floor this morning, and their XTRATUF rubber boots were on, they stuffed a quick breakfast and several cups of coffee into them while phone calls were made as they arranged for heavy equipment to load the gear that would be collected throughout the day onto the Ballad… as much as i wanted to go and help them throughout the day, i knew in my heart that i would both be in their way and in no condition to do the heavy work they would be doing… i knew and felt i was in good physical condition, but i still had 10 years on them plus absolutely no experience with the hard manual labor they would do… i still offered to go and help, but Derrick just smiled and told me someone had to stay on the boat in case gear arrived back before they did… i knew what he was trying to say and smiled in return… i had a life of teaching, really tough in many aspects but a world apart from the daily grind of a commercial fishermen… i often compared their hands to mine; their hands told of hardship and work my callous free hands had never seen… after a morning of hot coffee, eggs, and several pounds of bacon my friends left me to gather and organize the gear that would be needed to go king crabbing in Alaska…

with a free day to just nap, read, and wander in town i planned my day… i spent the morning in the wheelhouse sitting at the helm dreaming of a life i never had… life takes us on many journeys yet there are just not enough journeys for the dreams we all had… it was a funny twist of fate how i envied their journey, while they in return envied mine… i have always appreciated my blessings and given thanks for them always…

after a morning in which i read and napped—yes, i felt guilty thinking of the work my friends were doing—i also put on my XTRATUF boots and walked into town… with nowhere in particular to go i just walked and enjoyed the light rain that fell… morning passed into the afternoon and the afternoon passed without my friends returning… did they abandoned me on the boat and are now in some bar passing the time drinking and telling stories, but just as i was thinking those thoughts a large flatbed truck pulled up with a mountain of gear loaded on it… moments later a large truck with a crane pulled up beside the other truck… without even a hello, orders were being shouted and gear was being lifted into the Ballad… i asked Derrick if they needed help and he just gave me that smiled saying they had this under control… the late afternoon passed into early evening when finally boots were taken off signaling their work was done for the day… i now looked out on the deck of the Ballad that once held all the passengers… the seats were empty, but now large crab traps and literally miles of rope hid the seats from view… i was totally baffled at the amount of gear that was necessary just to do some crabbing… the traps loaded on board were just small 6 or 7 foot pyramid-like traps that weighed around 200 pounds compared to the big traps that weigh about 700 pounds and measure 7 by 7 by 3 feet that were used out in the Bering Sea…

we feasted on a dinner… believe me when i tell you that the refrigerators on the Ballad were well stocked for our trip… every type of meat from a selection of deli meats and cheeses for sandwiches, good old hot dogs to huge 10-pound roasts filled the refrigerators, plus every type of snack you could think of, and that included ice cream… Alaskan king crabbers are known for their love of ice cream and the amount they consumed during a crabbing season…

after dinner a movie on the tv filled in the silence while still more plans were being made for the next day… when asked if i had a nice day i didn't have the nerve to tell the of my naps and walks in the rain as i splashed through puddles like a child…

Feb 16, 2016
Ketchikan, Alaska

with the sky gray and Deer Mountain blanketed in clouds, the rain continued to fall… i wondered did it ever stop… i always wanted to spend a winter day like this in Ketchikan, and today my dream came true…the day was cold and damp with untouched puddles that covered the sidewalks… these sidewalk became small playgrounds for the boots of those who wandered aimlessly, without destination, other than a walk in a silent drizzle… it was a day that i found myself in the wheelhouse of the Ballad, i sat in my chair and read and napped as i saw fit… my morning also had a beautiful walk in this rain as it felt good to be cleansed by this winter shower… the boats sat idle in the harbors as they enjoyed a winter's sleep until the storms of spring … my eyes wandered to the many houses with windows overlooking the waterfront, i imagined how many chairs were placed by these windows with hungry eyes that soaked in these rainy days… with a pile of books by my side, a mug of hot tea, and wrapped in my blanket, i would have spent my Ketchikan days throughout this winter… and today was a beautiful day as my mind traveled through memories and the fantasies that i hoped would become a reality… visions that i waited a lifetime to come true, but along with those dreams were the nightmares of the uncertain days ahead…

but for my commercial fisherman friends it was another day of hard manual work but now in the rain… i couldn't believe that any more equipment would be necessary, but sure enough—i got back from my morning walk and my friends were unloading the final traps and lines necessary for our trip... with their wok finally finished, another great lunch was served… we feasted on hot pork sandwiches from the massive pork roast that Derrick prepared for us yesterday, and then Derrick headed out to the airport to pick up David Lethin, the owner of the Aleutian Ballad, as he would captain us during our crabbing in Ernest Sound about 50 nautical miles north of Ketchikan…

i knew David from previous years going on Princess Cruise's excursions on the Aleutian Ballad and both of us giving talks aboard Princess ships… David took us all down to the best local fish house in Ketchikan, rightly called the Ketchikan Fish House, where we all had the best fish tacos and chowder in town then after dinner we headed back to the boat, as tomorrow would come early…

Feb 19, 2016

Crabbing in Ernest Sound, Alaska

in the early hour of the morning, before the rising of the sun, the smell of diesel and the roar of the boat's engines filled the air as dock lines were secured on board and slowly the dock slipped away… although i wasn't working, i was now actually a crew member on a commercial crab boat heading out to catch a load of Alaskan king crabs…

i sat up in the pilot house and looked out on the deck watching Derrick, Andy, and Terry beginning to get all the crab traps and lines ready to be dropped in the water… crabbing tags from Alaska Game and Fish had to be secured to each trap, plus all the traps had to be baited prior to being put in the water… i watched the first set of traps being baited, and i knew that was one job i would be able to do… leaving the pilot house i approached Derrick with my suggestions and once again his smile told me, "jules just watch, as it's so easy to get seriously hurt", so with his smile i returned to the pilot house to talk with David and listen to his fishing stories from his crabbing days in Alaska…

now with the use of a computer linked to the ship's GPS and navigational charts, marking your course and location of each of the traps you drop makes the finding and retrieval of these traps much easier… as we approached the location for the first set of traps to be dropped, i listened to the communication between David, at the helm, and the crew that would soon drop the traps… once the first trap hit the water, it was just like watching *The Deadliest Catch,* but we were in the calm waters of Ernest Sound instead of the Bering Sea…

all throughout the day, in a light to sometimes heavy rain, i watched trap after trap being dropped… with each one that was dropped the crew had to also throw coils of lines that secured the traps in the water… each of those bundles of line probably weighed over 60 pounds, and not once did any of my friends hesitate picking up the weight and tossing it into the water… if that was me down there, and even if i was able to pick up the bulk of line, instead of tossing it 20 feet or more from the boat into the water, my throw would have been a sloppy drop straight over the side… i can't imagine how much weight the crew lifted that day and these were not young kids working, but men just a few years younger than me… after a set of traps were dropped, the crew got a short break as we moved to a new location, and then it all began again, trap after trap being dropped with its required length of line…this went on all throughout the day whether it was raining or not…

once the final set was dropped, i could see the exhaustion in my friends' faces and bodies… as they came into the cabin, wet and tired, i made sure i had coffee for each of them and a good hot BBQ pork sandwich… when i finally talked with Derrick, i smiled at him and told him he was right, i would have killed myself trying to work out there on the deck… Derrick smiled and said, "that's why you don't want to be a commercial fisherman, it's hard work and people do get seriously hurt"

Feb 18, 2016

Ketchikan, Alaska

with the crab traps down to soak (another way to say, waiting for the crabs to fill the traps) my fishermen friends packed their bags and flew back to Portland… they all would return in two weeks to haul the traps back in, hopefully loaded with crabs and then unload the gear for another year…

after they had all left for home, i would have another two days in Ketchikan before i too flew back home… all throughout the day my thoughts wandered to my friend Derrick… i think of the all the laughter and meals we shared in Alaska last summer … Derrick can make one hell of a grilled cheese sandwich, and we ate plenty of them throughout the summer… i was respected by Derrick, not only for my knowledge of Alaska, but also for the presentations i gave during the summer for Princess Cruises…. i was the naturalist that Derrick and the crew of the Aleutian Ballad loved and spoke accolades of… often Derrick and i would talk of our journeys through life… there was always respect shared for the paths that we each traveled down… and now, as i think of my future, once this ugly lie has been spoken… all i can see are floods of tears… my name being slandered… covered with mud… the ugly waves of gossip that will spread through my circle of friends in this little town of Ketchikan… a town where friends always brought summer smiles… will i have to let my shadow avoid these friends once they know…

Feb 19, 2016
Ketchikan, Alaska

enjoying and cherishing another day of solitude in Ketchikan… cold, damp and rainy; what more could i ask for… while the morning and afternoon showers quietly fell, i sat by a window with my mugs of tea and a sleeping bag as my blanket… finally my dream of spending a winter in Ketchikan has happened, thanks to Derrick, as i'm staying in his Ketchikan condo… i spent the afternoon hours reading and dreaming… when my eyes grew weary of words, i took to my raincoat and boots and walked the wet streets of this quiet town… the sidewalks are empty of the summer crowds so i could freely wander at will… the puddles were all mine to splash through as i walked with no destination in mind… i treasure the thought of another full day alone in my winter paradise, with nothing other than reading and walking in the rain before i must head for home…

i talked with Joanne on the phone and as we briefly talked about our tomorrows… i could still hear the pain in her voice as she admitted that she wishes this all would fade or go away… i battle

with my pain and frustration… the anticipation of a possible life-
long dream…

Feb 22, 2016
At home in Arizona

it's early in the morning and i sit in my chair and write… it feels so
good to be home… Joshua lays by my side… a lonely candle silently
burns… thoughts of my days on the Ballad… images of Ketchikan,
and then the hard decisions i must make… storms to be weathered,
all before i feel the calm again, if ever i will

Part 2:

Selections from:
Footsteps in Solitude

Thoughts of a Country
Far to the North

this was written after hiking on the ice cap in the interior of Greenland... the plane i was on landed, and its crew was taking supplies to Dye 3, a radar site that was a part of North America's early warning system... i spent several hours alone walking or wandering on the ice... these words are a reflection of my thoughts while out on the ice...

sounds from an empty world

sounds from an empty world
where the wind will journey over a
vastness not yet felt
and the only movement is between
the darkness and an empty twilight
snow, the wayfaring traveler,
lost and wandering
in a sea of ice.
sounds are never heard,
it's a world
without the need of touch, sound or sight
a yesterday which has no tomorrow
for time does not exist.
its presence can't be felt
its past cannot be seen
all is motionless without the images of life
beauty is lost in a vacant loneliness
where the eye can see
but only empty reflections of silence are felt
a voice can echo sounds of life

and be lost and forgotten before it was ever heard
where hope and dreams
have no value, no use
an eternity of emptiness
where the concept of time is meaningless
and can't be remembered
a graveyard filled with empty graves
for the dead have even abandoned this world
yet as i stand here
alone and with only my thoughts
i wonder my friend
what are you like
what are you like
under your skin
so thick
what are you like
what is hidden that will never be seen?

jtalarico
1975

Thoughts from the
Georgia Countryside

#1
i drifted down a carefree highway
muddled in warmth
by oaks
that shielded out the cold
while the sun's warmth
chanted encouragement
to my wandering spirit

the road folded gently
to the north
slowly the oaks faded
until
i left that carefree highway

the warmth
of the oaks were lost
i hesitated
thoughts of turning around
but i remembered
that this journey was not yet over

#2
a shower of colors
both faded and abandoned
forms lonely piles
that flood the roadside
this faded rainbow of cover

is now bidding us a good-bye

they will hold a child's fascination
but only for a moment
as they plow aimlessly amongst them
but soon they will be gone
the trees soon to be wrapped securely
in a blanket of white
called winter

#3
the serenity of the night
gently being stirred
leaves laying gently upon a pond
while a soft
mystifying fog silently slips in
dawn is awakening
and soon
its warmth will fondle us
morning dew
like crystals of ice
sparkle a choir of praise to this new dawn
the forest
mystical in this moment
hesitates in prayer
before lifting its arms
to the awaiting moments
must time go on...

#4
the warmth of a tree
has fallen

now
only to blanket the earth
for the tree now stands naked
its emptiness reaching into nowhere
winter
will soon embrace
clutching
cold and lonely
weighing upon that empty tree
until
a flower buds
then the warmth of summer can return

jtalarico
1979

Andersonville

granite monuments
damp, cold and lonely
stand guardian
amongst this army

i came
not as the others
for as i walked your ranks
alone
with thoughts and tears
i felt your pride and i stood with reverence

your numbers
so vast
quiet
i'm sorry
that i can't see
the reflections of death
and to take
but a moment of the pain
that touched you

i walked amongst your suffering
trying
but never able to touch
for the grass is soft and
i took that step
without fear or caution
for the lines no longer takes the brave

although now many pages
separate us
and i too wear a uniform
i wonder
could i lay
shoulder to shoulder
amongst my comrades
within an army
of cold stone

jtalarico
1979

Farewell to a Friend
Greenland 1975

the carrousel has stopped.
the music is no longer heard,
one more rider disembarks for yet another ride,
and only his memory can bring back
all of the laughter.
It's in these quiet moments,
the waiting
for the carrousel to begin again,
an empty silence,
waiting and wishing for our laughter to return
but it won't ever be the same again.
as our rider leaves,
so we get a new face,
can he fill the empty shoes,
i hope not
for it would ruin a fond memory.
the carrousel begins again.

jtalarico

Thinking of the Smokey Mountains while in Georgia

lovely lady
do you want to hold me
feel me
touch me
see me
and be with me

gentle hills
silhouetted in shades of blues and grays
the manzanitas
branches a reddish-bronze in color
flowered a trail
a trail marked by blazes
from those who walked this forest so long ago
their names have been lost
but their mark remains
remains for us to follow
within this forest of trees
eastern hemlock, white ash, sugar maple, yellow birch
and so many more
your trail was softened today
by leaves from a fall that has gently passed

i walked softly
my touch was gentle
for i saw you as a lady
a lady that i beg
to come with me
sit with me

share with me
love me
be my lovely lady

and lovely lady
with your mountains so high
caress me
yes i want you
i need you
to be within you

but whatever thoughts you have in mind
remember lady the mountains are mine

jtalarico
1978

Thinking of a Place that I Longed for, a Special Friend, the Grand Canyon

alone
with only thoughts
i gaze from this window
reaching
but never touching
for i long to belong again

my touch
is hungry
to feel your strength
like a child
to fondle
grasp
wonder
then only to let go
for i dare not disturb.

my sight
drifts aimlessly
although this window
is filled
filled with forms
i stare with emptiness
for the pastel of colors
soft and mystifying
that comfort and bring reverence
are no longer my reflections
i miss you my friend

jtalarico
1978

Walden

written in the cover of the book, *The Illustrated World of Thoreau,*
which was given as a gift to my mother…

a small bird
cautiously
creeps out on a distant limb,
it clings desperately
but with an unproven faith his instincts
tell him to let go,
so slowly
in a poetry of motion
he lifts his wings to the heavens
and begins to live.

and within this cover
are but a few pages
and cast upon them
are the wise words of a sensitive man.

maybe from them
you may find within yourself
a rock.
that you may find refuge on
and contemplate about
the happiness that you
have taught me to feel and that you
have given to me.

with much love
your son, Tal

jtalarico

230

Want Not I

thoughts after freeing my father's ashes into the canyon that he dearly loved, and words for me when i too become just a handful of ash… **words in the parentheses were added by my mother…**

a box of wood, lead
  or even bronze.
  a plot of earth
  confined and restless.
  a slab of granite
  cold and empty
  to tell my tale.
  placed in a land
  filled with death,
  sadness and tears.

instead give me the fire
  that helped warm me when chilled,
  fed me when hungry
  and comforted me while i loved.
  give me the fire
  its company that i enjoyed
  at night.
  peaceful campfires
  beauty
  blazing yet untouchable.
  let me be a part of that friend.
and when i have become but a
  handful of ash,
  free me once again
  on a mountain
  standing bold,

or over a canyon
filled with mystery
beauty
and solitude.

cast me free
so i may be the cool mountain breeze
the wings of an eagle
soaring free and proud.
cast me so i may be a
part of the river
creating and dancing free.
so i may solidify into rock
stand bold
a cathedral for belief.
be a part of the soil
that i have
walked,
felt
and loved.

cast me free
so i may be the meadows
filled with wildflowers
gentle
as i've tried to be.
let me be a part of the forest floor
a soft carpet of needles
that once graced a
redwood, cedar or hemlock.

cast me free
from a lonely and distant
summit
so that i can witness

and feel the harsh summit winds
and stand guardian
over my garden.

cast me free
upon the restless wind and endless sea
where the salt air blows
amongst the rhythm of the swells
and to countless shores
i shall drift
to the endless depths
i shall explore

cast me away
on a cool morning breeze
let me dance and be
a part of what i have loved....

for then (in God's will)
i will have truly lived (on)

jtalarico

Written for some Very Special Friends

this pair of boots
worn and soiled
but cared for
walked with
when i chose only my shadow for my company

and it's this pair of boots
with your tired touch
you showed me the desert solitude
mountain highs
we walked in the quiet rain
you helped me through the winter's snow
fields of wildflowers
canyons of rocks

this pair of boots
we walked along country roads
been drenched by the desert sun
you carried me through the miles
quiet, deserted trails
a rock by a river's bank

this pair of boots
you sat silently amongst my circle of friends
we passed a bottle
a warm, Indian fire burning
the laughter
you my friend, were a witness to my smiles

and it's always my boots
when the day is late
and the sun sinks low
and the mountain's solitude turns to a faded, grayish blue
against a tired evening sky
it's always my pair of boots
that will carry me home to you my love

jtalarico
written sometime in the mid 1970's

Selections from:
*After Footsteps
in Solitude*

To My Son: by Jeannie Talarico

my turbulent teenage years were filled with rebellion as i struggled
with finding out who i am, what i am… this was written to me, by
my mother as i left for college…

I can still feel the pain of it…
The thunder of our voices
Protesting, defending, clinging, pulling
And then…
I let you go!

Now you stand alone, Independent.
I am needed for some things, like…
Friendship.
And when you allow, the sharing of some dream.

In some small ways you let me mother you…
Sometimes I sew a button on
Match your socks
Or
Cook your favorite meal.

I know I must tread gently,
Your manhood is new…
And still a delicate thing.
You watch closely lest I take a part away,
But I like the man you seem to be…
Just as I liked the little boy you were.

I cannot know so much about you now.
Sometimes I wonder though…
Do you still cry?

I cannot help you if you do.
Now you must know your fantasies,
You will find life cruel…
And very, very sweet.
Always demanding to be lived

Stand tall…
Your will is strong, and after all
You remember ideals I taught!
Mix mine with your, and live life full…
Dare to know all parts of it.

Remember, man never knows his strength,
Until he knows his weaknesses.
Use these even well…
Turn them into strength or either will prevail…
It's just for you to decide.

So…
Go meet life.
Seed of my seed.
Do me some justice.
Yes, no matter what… You are still my beloved son.

Jennie Talarico
Copyright 1972

Tal's Reponse; To My Son

i wrote this in response to my mother's words… an answer to your
poem *To My Son* (1976)…

a restless wind
wandering contentedly
blowing a gentle breeze
and the sun being lowered
as tiny stars faithfully begin to shine
and make the night a place so peaceful
secure
to lay my weary thoughts down
though this path is long
and many suns will rise only to fall again
before i arrive
i will.

my hands are stronger now
for they hold the love i share and treasure
but are still young enough
to fondle the earth
and now you don't have to help with their cleaning
yes, they are bigger now
but then they can carry so much more happiness home
they don't move about awkwardly
searching for the rhythm to securely tie the bows
so shoestrings won't
follow in the lagging shadow of
is it true
a man.

my shoes
dusty, tired
lay resting awaiting the mornings early call
they have grown so much in the years
to help find the path through life
the toes are still scoffed
as often life is so sweet
i drag myself slowly through the minutes
do you want to pick them up again
as you have so many times before
but you hesitate
as you know they are finding the way to manhood.

still another pair of faded
worn and soiled jeans
but they too are so big
you wonder
are your steps into life that hard
that you need legs so much bigger than before
who puts the patches on the knees now
for the minutes you stop to share
on your knees in a world i know not of
how many patches do you go through now
before you lay your jeans aside,
now for a new source of patches for yet another pair of jeans
do you want to fold them
lay them by my bed
for yet another day
i don't mind
for they will enjoy your forgotten touch again.

why do you stare
so different
has my face sadden you

yes my eyes are still chocolate
but do I see a tear in yours
i know they aren't the eyes of a child
for they are seeing the world of a man now
and they grow tired at times
and close to see the dreams only I have shared
in lonely and troubled times
but they haven't grown to the extent that
tears of happiness won't flow from them
do they look wiser
they're really not
for they still seek new and curious things
it could be the love in them
for they often stare at a woman
yes and her body is so soft and beautiful
even though I lay
with my eyes closed now
and you stand there so quietly watching me
i think I know what has sadden you
it's the image of this man.

when i awake
to walk into another day
do i stand too tall
i know you look upon me with questions
what ideals do i still hold
are there many new ones
which ones have been left aside by my hastened pace
i never feel that big though
i know i stand so tall
but I still look up to you
so even though you stretch up
and I lower myself down
as you often did

and you lay gently upon my cheek
in the ways of a mother
who wants to hold on a little longer
and enjoy caring once again for this child
a kiss
don't cry mom
for even though you set me free
i'll always know my way home again.

jtalarico

Denali

dogs are said to be man's best friend… a perfect example of unconditional love… they give to you so much joy, and it hurts like hell when they leave… you swear never again… but could i ever live without their presence…

February 14, 2014

how do you say good bye… is it even possible… for 16 years she blessed us every day with her love… she was always there… yet as i look around the house, all her favorite little spots… now they are empty… the house feels empty… i feel empty… and i hurt… i would do anything just to feel her one more time… i wonder will this pain ever go away… do i want it to leave… for then, would i no longer feel her loss…

my mind races through memories… i try to recreate all the joy we had because of her… i look at her little red bowl… her favorite pillow in her later years, her toys… emptiness now and pain… the house is filled with empty shadows… i'm afraid to call her name because i know only silence will follow… she trusted me… did i fail her in the end… i have to believe i did what was best for her for she gave me everything… she trusted my love…

when we walked away… we left her lying there… she looked so peaceful… she was beautiful… even though her poor little body showed her age and her fading health, i'll carry that last image of her always in my heart…

i'll miss you always Josie…

Josie was the sixth dog that left us… they were all special and added to our joy… and each brought its own pain… some i tried to put to ink…

to Denali… my friend… my dog

lying on that table
scared
and only a shadow of what once was
the look you gave
said you didn't understand
but my touch you trusted
i was there for your pain
but did you understand.

i had to let you go
say good-bye
and walk away alone
yet i just don't know how to say good-by

our time was short
and my memories are many
yet as i search the house through and through
only to find your fading scent
and to call your name now
and to hear only an empty echo
a part of me is gone

i had to let you go
say good-bye
and walk away alone
yet i just don't know how to say good-bye

the days have passed and gone
and by my feet he sleeps
he gently took your shadow's place
and touched my sadden heart

for this was your final gift to me

i had to let you go
say good-bye
and walk away alone
yet i just don't know how to say good-bye

jtalartico

A selection from:
Alaskan Thoughts

Dreams

i realized today that when i said "my dreams", yes i was dealing with getting older and my mortality, but also in part, my dreams were dealing with a dark secret… growing older with time slipping by… this was written in June, just 5 months before my life as jules ended… i had no idea that i would ever make my dark secret known, let alone act on it… i always believed my dream was only a broken dream that would never happen…
thoughts of growing old and facing my mortality…

i'm Ketchikan bound
and dreams, they are chasing me
scaring me through this night,
and yet their cries of joy still echo all through this sleepless night
my window to this world was thrown open
a broken twilight comforts me
it paints that world that i love
that i cry for
am i blessed or cursed
do i really know
thoughts and visions dance through my sleepless state
and yet i'm scared
i grow older
i want to grab out and cling
hold on to this blessing called youth
i want to sweat again
rest on a rock and cry out in joy
i want to feel fear racing through my blood
i want to lay and feel her heart beat
be covered by your scent
a candle flickers in our darkened room
we lay naked

side by side
i want to mold memories that won't rust in time
for i feel my shelves are still only half full
all those books that call out for my weary eyes and
cry for my hands to caress their pages
i want to feel the loss of throwing out boots that carried me through
endless journeys
smell the leather bathed in my sweat
Joshua
i want to look into your big brown eyes
feel your unconditional love
to see your shadow walk with mine…

and i cry
i cry for those tranquility days are gone
damn it, why did i let them slip away in the night
do we ever know our blessings until they are stolen from our grasp
you tell me there are others to be had
the hell with you
for i will never be able to replace perfection
she was mine
and she's gone
god i love
no i hate these memories
does the pain of loss feel good
does it bronze those lost memories forever

part II

it's 4 in the morning and my spirit is restless
tormented by words that scream out to be felt
to be written
the wind sings a haunting song as i stand on a lonely deck bathed in
the tears of dew

my favorite sweatshirt
worn from use
hugs me in a feeling of warmth as this new day unfolds
i love this loneliness of dawn
solitude that is all mine
i'm selfish
i want to steal these moments so they are mine alone
the sky is undecided between the gray clouds and a broken blue
the forest
still a shadow of green that floats by ever so slowly
i wonder do these islands have names
do they really need a label placed upon their shoulders
a burden they must carry on the charts of those who live on this sea
a new day begins to dawn
the mountains drift by
my heart and soul cry out to these broken dreams of mine
and these dreams will they heal this broken body
keep my hands grasping
clinging
keep me dreaming
for my dreams are my tomorrows
and my todays
well they always become my yesterdays

part III

my mortality
it stares at me every day
i often hear, "your life has been blessed, you've done so much"
but i am restless
where has my youth gone
often my body says "no i can't do that anymore"
but my dreams are defiant, i cannot let them rust
my summers in Alaska are bittersweet

i want so much more
will i regret these days passively watching this coast with these
mountains drifting by
ah, these dreams
are they curses or my tomorrows…
it's 3 in the morning
but it could just as well be noon
for my dreams are restless
restless as this ship drifts
through a maze of time
are we northbound or southbound
hell, does really doesn't matter
for this restlessness is devouring me
while i'm chasing dreams
and of time
well it doesn't stand still in this void
no, no it's stealing my precious years
time that i need to chase my dreams
dreams that are taken from memories worn thin
from the many lonely moments
moments that became my thoughts
thoughts that once again fade into new dreams
my boots sit tossed in a closet
restless for a path to wander
they cry to be muddied, and washed in sweat
instead of the dust that slowly covers
a face that also cries for more time…

i regretfully finish yet another book
i cling to its essence
i cry "why must you end, my friend"
a book that stirred more dreams than time will allow
and of the books that still await my hands
are they too filled with dreams

and i ponder
are these books filled with curses
curses rather than dreams
the curses caused by my fading years
journeys that will never be taken
and it's then that i hear my spirit scream
it's restless in these empty hours that pass
and as i sit and watch this canvas painted
painted with mountains that i can't touch
i can almost feel the tranquility of its forest
being wrapped in that cocoon of green
ah my essence cries in restless desperation
and time passes slowly by…

my summers
yes they are bittersweet
i do love the sea
for as Dana spoke
"nothing will compare with the early breaking of day upon the wide
ocean"
i love the taste of the salt in the air
a wind and sea that are alive
but my heart cries as i stand watch
and a coastline silently passes
i want my kayak days back again
i did not walk this coastline
for it is not a part of my memory of time
and of time
well it's 3 in the morning
but it could just as well be noon
for my dreams are restless
restless as this ship drifts
drifts through a maze of time

jtalarico
June 30, 2015

CPSIA information can be obtained
at www.ICGtesting.com
Printed in the USA
LVHW040153210722
723934LV00001B/52